EDWARD'S MENAGERIE
BIRDS

#edsanimals

ABOUT THE AUTHOR

Kerry Lord is the founder of TOFT, a dynamic British yarn brand specialising in luxury wools and approachable patterns. Initially established with a focus on fashion-led knitting kits, Kerry first created the first edition of this very popular *Edward's Menagerie* series of book in 2012, which has encouraged and taught thousands around the world to crochet for the first time.

Kerry enjoys collaborating and co-hosting ever-larger crochet events to bring people together that have TOFT in common, and introduce new people to the craft.

Find the videos recorded to accompany these patterns on the TOFT YouTube channel.

BE SOCIAL

Follow Kerry on most social media channels using @toft_uk to see more of her adventures in crochet.

One of the most exciting things about crocheting is joining the active online community helping and inspiring each other every day in their shared hobby. Share your makes using the tag **#edsanimals** to join in.

www.toftuk.com

EDWARD'S MENAGERIE
BIRDS

Over 50 easy-to-make soft toy bird crochet patterns

Kerry Lord

DAVID & CHARLES
—PUBLISHING—

www.davidandcharles.com

CONTENTS

ABOUT THE AUTHOR   2

BE SOCIAL   2

INTRODUCTION   7

HOW TO USE THIS BOOK   8

YOU WILL NEED   10

SIZE OPTIONS   12

STANDARD FORMS   14

PATTERNS

LEVEL 1

ERNEST the Canary   22

DAVE the Gull   24

DUKE the Mallard   26

CELINE the Dove   28

SOPHIA the Flamingo   30

VINCE the Blue-Footed Booby   32

DORA the Wood Pigeon   34

INA the Stork   36

DESMOND the Blue Tit   38

ALAN the Magpie   40

BARNEY the Barn Owl   42

HUCK the Pelican   44

ETHEL the Kiwi   46

JACOB the Hoopoe   48

LEVEL 2

HENRY the Raven   52

RORY the Northern Cardinal   54

MARGOT the Swan   56

HAZEL the Hen   58

ARTHUR the Blue-Winged Teal   60

ORLANDO the Roseate Spoonbill   62

PEDRO the Wine-Throated Hummingbird   64

ROSS the Turkey   66

ELIZABETH the Dodo   68

FLORIAN the Ostrich   70

EMILY the Vulture   72

DUDLEY the Red Grouse   74

ZANE the Grey Crowned Crane   76

ABRAHAM the Bald Eagle   78

KEVIN the Cassowary   80

TRAVIS the Pink Robin   82

TRICIA the Silkie Chicken   84

LEVEL 3

ELVIS the Cockatoo   88

MEGHAN the Toucan   90

ROBIN the Robin   92

JORGE the Jay   94

GARETH the Puffin   96

BEN the Kingfisher   98

YOLANDA the Cockatiel   100

GIANNI the Lovebird   102

PUTU the Lesser Bird Of Paradise   104

JACK the Macaw   106

RENÉE the Shalow's Turaco   108

TERENCE the Budgerigar   110

ENID the Long-Eared Owl   112

EZRA the Gouldian Finch   114

ROHIT the Peacock   116

LEVI the Red And Yellow Barbet   118

AGATHA the Vulturine Guinea Fowl   120

RAEGAN the King Penguin   122

CALLAHAN the Yokohama Cockerel   126

TECHNICALS

BASIC SKILLS   130

ABBREVIATIONS   131

WORKING THE STITCHES   132

FINISHING TECHNIQUES   136

MAKE YOUR TAIL FEATHERS   137

STUFFING AND SEWING   138

THANK YOU   142

SUPPLIERS   142

INTRODUCTION

Much as Bridget the Elephant and all her friends in the menagerie were first created for my newly born son, Edward, I think that *Edward's Menagerie: Birds* was made for me.

In the decade since I first designed Sophia the Flamingo these huge characters with their knobbly knees and crooked beaks have never stopped making me smile. They are bold, bright and beautiful and most are relatively quick makes, which make them perfect for gifting. I've had a canary, peacock and cockerel on my kitchen shelf for many years and they bring a big splash of colour into the room and proudly show–off my love of crochet.

Birds by their very appearance were always going to be a bit more fiddly than the original *Edward's Menagerie* mammals. That gawky yet somehow elegant avian character lends itself to small rounds and detailed shaping. I knew it would be more of a challenge with new shapes, big features and bright colours – but what I didn't know was that it could take TOFT off in a whole new colourful direction. The introduction of our first six brightly coloured yarns with which to hook up the first birds ten years ago has now expanded to include 18 more, making this book my most colourful yet with a tremendous 36 colours used in the 50 projects.

If you are a complete beginner to crochet and *Edward's Menagerie*, then start with the Level 1 bird Ernest the Canary, who just uses the double crochet stitch and one simple colour change. In *Edward's Menagerie: Birds* the projects are arranged by difficulty, not only into levels, but also within that level, so you can progress through the pages onto those that require a bit more concentration and new techniques such as loop stitch.

The patterns in this book are designed for you and your friends and family to enjoy and are for personal use only. I love seeing photos of your menagerie birds; make sure you share them using the hashtag #edsanimals, so that I can enjoy looking at them, and you can see everyone else's, too.

It has been an absolute pleasure to revisit and expand my *Edward's Menagerie* aviary and I know that these bird patterns will bring a lot of joy not just to you when you are making them, but also to anyone who happens to see you doing so.

Have fun!

Kerry

HOW TO USE THIS BOOK

Edward's Menagerie: Birds has been divided into three levels to indicate how many techniques are used in the making of that bird, and are arranged within those levels with those that are the most challenging or longest makes towards the end of each section. Level 1 birds do include simple colour changing where you move from one ball to the next once within a piece, but other than that it's just the basics of increasing and decreasing with the double crochet stitch.

LEVEL 1

The birds in Level 1 use only chain, slip stitch, double crochet, and basic colour changes moving cleanly from one colour to another. Cut your yarn after the change if you have fully finished using the first colour, leaving a short end. There is no need to sew or tie ends in, simply leave them inside the piece. If you are moving back and forth between two colours such as creating stripes, then drop the colour not in use and pick it back up when you return to it. The floats will run along the inside of the piece. Level 1 birds are suitable for beginners who refer to the *Technicals* section as they learn.

LEVEL 2

To make the Level 2 birds you will need a few extra skills including learning the half treble and treble stitches, how to make a bobble, and towards the end of this level you will master the loop stitch. Loop stitches can be left as loops or cut once completed to create a different texture on the bird.

LEVEL 3

Level 3 birds require complex colour changing patterns that are demanding to follow in addition to the shaping so it's advisable to have made at least one other bird from the other levels before embarking on these patterns if you are a beginner. Within Level 3 patterns you will move backwards and forwards between colours, stranding the unused yarn within the piece. All birds using the CLIMBING legs are within this level as using a chain to split the round and change direction can take a bit of getting used to the first time you do it.

Please don't feel that you have to practise, learn or master the *Technicals* section of this book before you dive head-first into a project. Flick to the back as you go along to acquire, double check or refresh your skills as you work through your first bird.

The birds in this book are of a feather and share common body shapes. You will need to refer to the *Standard Forms* pages when making any of them and the pattern page will give specific instruction on using the standard form patterns to create longer necks, shorter legs and the odd hairy foot. You will notice that these pages have a pink tab to help you find them quickly when you are working through a pattern. After you have made one bird, you will pick up the pattern quickly (and become very familiar with your six times table!).

If you are totally new to crochet then get your hook in with a Level 1 bird first and then you'll quickly progress onto the penguin, peacock and parrots!

To keep each pattern simple and concise, I have omitted the stuffing and the sewing-up instructions, as these are common to all. Please refer to the *Stuffing and Sewing* pages in the *Technicals* section before you start, so that you are aware of the easiest order to do this. These pages have a raspberry tab.

The patterns all use British crochet terminology and common crochet abbreviations. US conversions and full explanations can be found in the *Technicals* section.

YOU WILL NEED

MY YARN CHOICE

Edward's Menagerie: Birds has been crocheted entirely in TOFT double knitting pure wool yarn on a 3mm hook. This collection of bird patterns showcases the soft handle of natural fibres, the depth and boldness of fibre-dyed colours and the tactile appeal of the resulting fabric.

The creation of *Edward's Menagerie: Birds* in 2015 pushed the TOFT brand in a new direction, spinning our first bright dyed yarns, and that has continued to expand to the 36 colours used in this book. Naturally, I recommend using TOFT yarn to guarantee that your birds look and feel just like mine, but the patterns will work in any other non-fancy spun yarn. The resulting birds will vary drastically should you choose to work up a bleached white acrylic dove or an owl in bright pink cotton, but the patterns will work if you match your hook size to your yarn and check that your tension makes a dense, crisp fabric.

YARN COLOURS

The birds in this book have been made using a palette of 36 colours: 12 naturals, 12 bold bright primary and secondary shades, and then 12 more subtle shades often sharing the same tones. All 36 colours have been designed to tonally fit together and complement each other. The simplest birds use only two colours, but even the most humble of birds are very colourful and Callahan the Yokohama Cockerel boasts ten! The birds in this book use far more colours than anything else I have ever made or designed, and in making them I have discovered the pleasure in highlighting the neutrals I know so well with bright flashes. The only drawback to this is you will need a couple of balls of yarn in lots of different colours to get started, but then know they will all come in handy as you hook through the whole book.

MATERIALS FOR STUFFING

I choose to stuff these birds with a premium recycled polyester toy stuffing. If you are making these animals for children then this synthetic filling may be the most practical option as it makes them fully hand-washable. However, I do often use pure wool and plant-based cotton and kapok stuffing when making the birds for adults to enjoy as mascots in their homes or at work as an all-natural more environmental choice.

MATERIALS FOR FACES

I have used Black yarn to sew on all the birds' eyes. Alternatively, you could use buttons, beads or safety eyes if you wish, adding these in before you do final sewing up. Do not use safety eyes, buttons, beads or glass eyes on toys intended for children under three years old as they are a potential choking hazard; securely embroider the features instead as I have done so.

TO MAKE JUST ONE, OR INDEED ALL, OF THE BIRDS IN THIS BOOK, THE REQUIREMENTS LIST IS THE SAME:

Yarn in appropriate colours and quantities (see *Size Options* and each project)

One hook in an appropriate size to the yarn being used (see *Size Options*)

A scrap of yarn or stitch marker to keep track of your progress

Stuffing material

Black contrast yarn for eyes

Scissors

Sewing needle

Modelling wire (optional)

COLOURS ABOVE
(from left to right, top to bottom)

Primrose, Coral, Ruby,
Yellow, Apricot, Beetroot,
Sapphire, Kale, Sage,
Lime, Chive, Green,
Fudge, Chestnut, Cocoa,
Oatmeal, Camel, Mushroom

COLOURS ABOVE
(from left to right, top to bottom)

Peach, Peony, Raspberry,
Orange, Pink, Magenta,
Violet, Hyacinth, Turquoise,
Amethyst, Blue, Teal,
Shale, Steel, Charcoal,
Cream, Silver, Stone

SIZE OPTIONS

The standard *Edward's Menagerie* bird shown on each project page is worked in TOFT pure wool double knitting (DK) weight yarn on a 3mm crochet hook (for US crocheters: light worsted/8ply yarn on a C2 or D3 hook). The beauty of the pattern is that you never need to change the hook size and you need only one tool to make all 50 birds featured in this book!

All the figures given here are approximate and based on my experience in working with TOFT yarns.

You could make any one of these birds in any thickness of yarn, but with the Level 3 birds you may find some techniques (and the sewing up) becomes quite demanding when worked in very fine yarns. Thicker yarns and bigger hooks often suit beginners best, as it can be less fiddly and is easier to see the stitches.

Yarn quantities are based on using TOFT pure wool yarn. If you use another brand, the quantities required may vary significantly depending on the composition of the yarn. Birds that use the loop stitch or chain loops to add details, such as Tricia the Silkie Chicken or Ethel the Kiwi, will take considerably more yarn than others.

Your hook size needs to be selected based on yarn thickness but also considering your own personal tension. Adjust your hook size to accommodate your tension and thickness of yarn, ensuring that your fabric is dense: if it is too loose your stuffing will show through; if it is too tight your animals will be stiff and hard to work. The tension measurements opposite are approximate and measured over standard double crochet stitches worked in a spiral.

The size given in the box is for a standard body and perching leg bird measured standing to the top of its head – all head crests, long tails and feathers are additional to this.

INTERNATIONAL TERMS

I have used British English crochet terms throughout. 'Double crochet' (dc) is the same as the American English 'single crochet' (sc). For clarification on which stitch this refers to and for any additional abbreviations, see the instructions in the *Technicals* section.

SMALL		
YARN WEIGHT	UK	FINE (half a strand of DK)
	US/AU	SPORT/4PLY
QUANTITY	G	20–30
	OZ	¾–1
HOOK SIZE	MM	2
	US/AU	A
FINISHED SIZE	CM	18
	IN	7
TENSION	CM	2 x 2cm = 7 sts x 8 rnds
	IN	¾ x ¾in = 7 sts x 8 rnds

STANDARD		
YARN WEIGHT	UK	DK
	US/AU	LIGHT WORSTED/8PLY
QUANTITY	G	60–100
	OZ	2–3½
HOOK SIZE	MM	3
	US/AU	C2/D3
FINISHED SIZE	CM	24
	IN	9½
TENSION	CM	3 x 3cm = 6 sts x 7 rnds
	IN	1¼ x 1¼in = 6 sts x 7 rnds

LARGE		
YARN WEIGHT	UK	ARAN (2 strands of DK)
	US/AU	WORSTED/10PLY
QUANTITY	G	200–400
	OZ	7–14
HOOK SIZE	MM	5
	US/AU	H8
FINISHED SIZE	CM	40
	IN	15¾
TENSION	CM	5 x 5cm = 6 sts x 7 rnds
	IN	2 x 2in = 6 sts x 7 rnds

GIANT		
YARN WEIGHT	UK	CHUNKY (4 strands of DK)
	US/AU	BULKY/12PLY
QUANTITY	G	600–1000
	OZ	20–35
HOOK SIZE	MM	8
	US/AU	L11
FINISHED SIZE	CM	60
	IN	23½
TENSION	CM	7 x 7cm = 6 sts x 7 rnds
	IN	2¾ x 2¾in = 6 sts x 7 rnds

SIZE ORDER (from left to right) Small, Standard, Large, Giant

STANDARD FORMS

For this collection of bird patterns I have developed standard forms to cover certain shapes which are repeated within the patterns. I have labelled the parts as some patterns will require that you extend or reduce a section and this should make it really easy to visualise the subtle change to the standard form.

The bodies are created using a standard increase from a starting circle adding six stitches evenly into each round to create a flat hexagonal piece of crochet, worked in a spiral from the centre outwards. All legs are worked from the thighs downwards, tails from the body to the tip and beaks from the heads to the tips which means they all begin with an open chain start that you then crochet into to create the first round.

When you have completed a part, unless it is otherwise stated, break the yarn leaving at least 20cm (8in) with which you can sew up and pull it off the hook. I choose to stuff all parts once I have completed crocheting them, and so there is no need to do this as you go along unless it is stated in the patten before decreasing to a pointed finish. See also the *Stuffing and Sewing* and the *Make Your Tail Feathers* sections in *Technicals* for further advice on this.

For a more detailed explanation of the techniques, including how to start, how to work the stitches and changing colours, please refer to the *Technicals* section.

COUNTING

A basic skill to get yourself out of trouble is counting the number of stitches at the end of a round. After each round involving decreasing or increasing instructions, the number at the end in brackets will indicate how many stitches you should now have to work with. If you complete a round and this number is incorrect, simply pull back the round to your marker on the previous round and rework it.

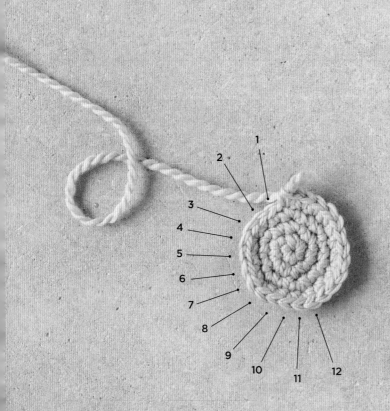

BODY/NECK/HEAD

In some patterns containing colour changing on the body and face of a bird you will move your end of round stitch marker when stated to make the colour changing simpler in combination with the shaping. This will be stated as RESET Rnd and your next line of instructions should be worked from this new position (even if in reality it is only partially through the previous round).

TIP

As you're crocheting the body clip a centraliser marker into the fifth decrease of rnd 22. This marks the centre of the chest to provide a guide for lining up the wings, legs and beak.

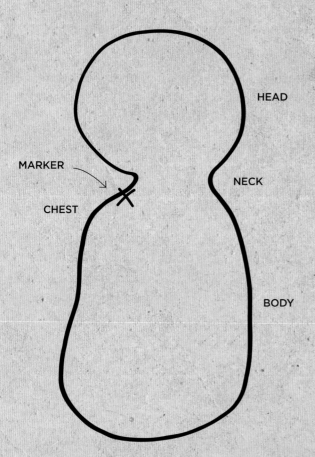

MARKER

CHEST

HEAD

NECK

BODY

BODY

Begin by dc6 into ring
Rnd 1 (dc2 into next st) 6 times (12)
Rnd 2 (dc1, dc2 into next st) 6 times (18)
Rnd 3 (dc2, dc2 into next st) 6 times (24)
Rnd 4 (dc3, dc2 into next st) 6 times (30)
Rnd 5 (dc4, dc2 into next st) 6 times (36)
Rnd 6 (dc5, dc2 into next st) 6 times (42)
Rnds 7-9 dc (3 rnds)
Rnd 10 (dc5, dc2tog) 6 times (36)
Rnds 11-14 dc (4 rnds)
Rnd 15 (dc4, dc2tog) 6 times (30)
Rnds 16-19 dc (4 rnds)
Rnd 20 (dc3, dc2tog) 6 times (24)
Rnd 21 dc
Rnd 22 dc3, (dc2tog) 9 times, dc3 (15)
Rnd 23 dc3, (dc2tog) 5 times, dc2 (10)

NECK

Rnd 1 dc

HEAD

Rnd 1 (dc2 into next st) 10 times (20)
Rnd 2 (dc3, dc2 into next st) 5 times (25)
Rnd 3 (dc4, dc2 into next st) 5 times (30)
Rnd 4 (dc2, dc2 into next st) 10 times (40)
Rnds 5-7 dc (3 rnds)
Rnd 8 (dc8, dc2tog) 4 times (36)
Rnd 9 dc
Rnd 10 (dc4, dc2tog) 6 times (30)
Rnd 11 (dc3, dc2tog) 6 times (24)
Rnd 12 (dc2, dc2tog) 6 times (18)
Rnd 13 dc
Rnd 14 (dc2tog) 9 times (9)
Stuff and gather remaining stitches to close.

LEGS

Most birds' legs are skinny, long and a little bit bony. Although you may find the small rounds a bit fiddly to begin with, it will get easier, but please ensure that you are working right-side out (RS vs. WS see *Technicals* for details). You will find it almost impossible to work a six stitch round inside out and you won't be able to flip it to the right side at the end as you can with larger parts.

To avoid having to create lots of very fiddly small parts that you then sew together the legs and toes are made in one piece, only breaking yarn at the tip of a toe before rejoining to work the next ones alongside.

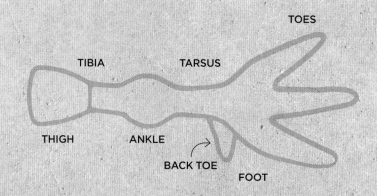

SPLITTING ROUNDS FOR PERCHING, PADDLING, GRASPING AND SWIMMING

Once the main foot has been worked as a continuation of the leg, the three toes are split off the main round to be worked flat side-by-side with each other. To do this, count the stated number of stitches backwards from your live stitch at the end of the foot and cross the round to double crochet into the front of that stitch. This forms the first round to work the first toe. Break yarn once completed. To work the second toe flat alongside this first one, rejoin the yarn into the last worked stitch and double crochet half the number of stated stitches along the main round away from the first toe you have made, then cross to the other side and work the other half of the stitches back towards the first toe to create a round upon which to work the second toe, breaking yarn once completed. Finally, rejoin and work the remaining stitches as the third and final toe. Sew in all the ends.

WORKING A BACK TOE ON PERCHING AND GRASPING

To make the foot three dimensional a back toe is worked at a right angle to the legs. To avoid having to securely sew on a small piece of crochet this can be directly crocheted into place into slip stitches traversed onto the surface of the foot. Alternatively you could work a 'dc6 into ring' (see *Technicals*) and crochet as a separate toe that you would then sew into place on the back of the foot at the base of the leg. This could also be left off if so wished.

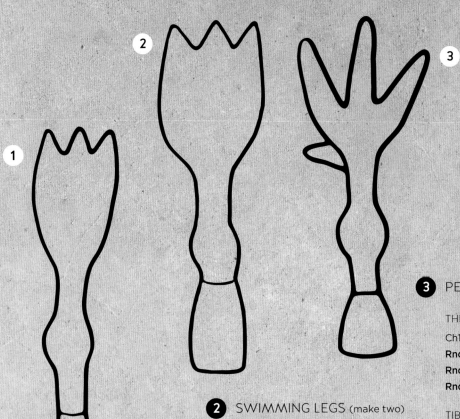

3 **PERCHING LEGS** (make two)

THIGH

Ch12 and sl st to join into a circle
Rnds 1-3 dc (3 rnds)
Rnd 4 (dc2, dc2tog) 3 times (9)
Rnd 5 (dc1, dc2tog) 3 times (6)

TIBIA

Rnds 1-5 dc (5 rnds)

ANKLE

Rnd 1 (dc2 into next st) 6 times (12)
Rnds 2-3 dc (2 rnds)
Rnd 4 (dc2tog) 6 times (6)

TARSUS

Rnds 1-5 dc (5 rnds)

FOOT

Rnd 1 (dc2 into next st) 6 times (12)
Rnd 2 (dc1, dc2 into next st) 6 times (18)

TOES

Split into three rnds of 6 sts and work
each as follows:
Rnds 1-3 dc (3 rnds)
Rnd 4 dc2tog, dc4 (5)
Rnds 5-6 dc (2 rnds)
Rnd 7 dc2tog, dc3 (4)
Break yarn.

BACK TOE

SLIP STITCH TRAVERSE a 6-st ring on
back of foot and work as follows:
Rnd 1 dc
Rnd 2 dc2tog, dc4 (5)
Rnds 3-4 dc (2 rnds)
Rnd 5 dc2tog, dc3 (4)
Break yarn.

Lightly stuff thigh and sew flat across
top to close.

2 SWIMMING LEGS (make two)

THIGH

Ch16 and sl st to join into a circle
Rnds 1-5 dc (5 rnds)
Rnd 6 (dc2, dc2tog) 4 times (12)
Rnd 7 (dc1, dc2tog) 4 times (8)

TIBIA

Rnds 1-2 dc (2 rnds)

ANKLE

Rnd 1 (dc1, dc2 into next st) 4 times (12)
Rnds 2-3 dc (2 rnds)
Rnd 4 (dc1, dc2tog) 4 times (8)

TARSUS

Rnds 1-7 dc (7 rnds)

FOOT

Rnd 1 (dc2 into next st) 8 times (16)
Rnd 2 dc
Rnd 3 (dc7, dc2 into next st) twice (18)
Rnd 4 (dc8, dc2 into next st) twice (20)
Rnd 5 dc
Rnd 6 (dc9, dc2 into next st) twice (22)
Rnd 7 dc
Rnd 8 (dc10, dc2 into next st) twice (24)
Rnds 9-11 dc (3 rnds)
Split into three rnds of 8 sts and work
each as follows:
Rnd 1 dc
Rnd 2 (dc2tog) 4 times (4)
Rnd 3 (dc2tog) twice (2)
Break yarn.

Lightly stuff thigh and foot and sew flat
across top to close.

1 PADDLING LEGS (make two)

Ch15 and sl st to join into a circle
Rnds 1-2 dc (2 rnds)
Rnd 3 (dc3, dc2tog) 3 times (12)
Rnd 4 (dc2, dc2tog) 3 times (9)
Rnds 5-6 dc (2 rnds)
Rnd 7 (dc1, dc2tog) 3 times (6)
Rnds 8-12 dc (5 rnds)
Rnd 13 (dc2 into next st) 6 times (12)
Rnds 14-15 dc (2 rnds)
Rnd 16 (dc2tog) 6 times (6)
Rnds 17-22 dc (6 rnds)
Rnd 23 (dc2 into next st) 6 times (12)
Rnd 24 dc
Rnd 25 (dc5, dc2 into next st) twice (14)
Rnd 26 (dc6, dc2 into next st) twice (16)
Rnd 27 (dc7, dc2 into next st) twice (18)
Rnds 28-32 dc (5 rnds)
Split into three rnds of 6 sts and work
each as follows:
Rnd 1 dc
Rnd 2 (dc2tog) 3 times (3)
Break yarn.

Lightly stuff thigh and sew flat across
top to close.

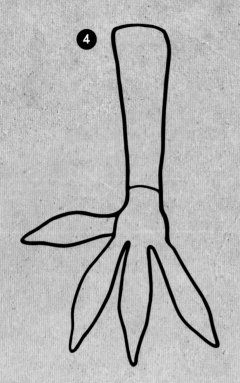

CREATING A RIGHT ANGLE WITH A CHAIN SPLIT

To create the 'T' shape in these legs at the base of the foot we make a chain that we then work into either side of to totally alter the direction of the round. When working the first round of 8 stitches following the chain work the 2 clear stitches from the round and then 6 stitches from the chain. When splitting the round after Rnd 2 of the foot, to get the neatest results you need these two 6-stitch rounds to sit flat alongside each other, so if your live stitch is not in the centre of the leg when you have completed Rnd 2 then double crochet a couple of extra stitches to get into this position before counting 6 stitches backwards to split this first round.

When rejoining following completing the first two toes you will be crocheting into the other side of the chain you made to split the rounds (2 off the bottom of the leg and 6 off the chain).

4 GRASPING LEGS (make two)

Ch15 and sl st to join into a circle
Rnds 1-2 dc (2 rnds)
Rnd 3 (dc3, dc2tog) 3 times (12)
Rnds 4-5 dc (2 rnds)
Rnd 6 (dc2, dc2tog) 3 times (9)
Rnds 7-12 dc (6 rnds)
Rnd 13 dc7, dc2tog (8)
Rnds 14-17 dc (4 rnds)
Rnd 18 (dc2 into next st) 8 times (16)
Rnd 19 (dc7, dc2 into next st) twice (18)
Split into three rnds of 6 sts and work each as follows:
Rnds 1-4 dc (4 rnds)
Rnd 5 dc5, dc2 into next st (7)
Rnd 6 dc
Rnd 7 dc6, dc2 into next st (8)
Rnd 8 dc
Rnd 9 (dc2tog) 4 times (4)
Rnd 10 dc
Rnd 11 (dc2tog) twice (2)
Break yarn.

BACK TOE

SLIP STITCH TRAVERSE a 6-st ring on back of foot and work as follows:
Rnds 1-3 dc (3 rnds)
Rnd 4 (dc1, dc2tog) twice (4)
Rnd 5 dc
Rnd 6 (dc2tog) twice (2)
Break yarn.

Lightly stuff thigh and sew flat across top to close.

5 CLIMBING LEGS (make two)

Ch12 and sl st to join into a circle
Rnds 1-8 dc (8 rnds)
Rnd 9 (dc2tog) 6 times (6)
Rnds 10-18 dc (9 rnds)
Next, ch6 and sl st across to other side of rnd to form two 8-st rnds at right angles to the leg when working either side of the chain.

FOOT

Work each rnd as follows:
Rnd 1 dc8 (2 from rnd, 6 on chain)
Rnd 2 (dc1, dc2 into next st) 4 times (12)

TOES

Split into two rnds of 6 sts and work each as follows:
Rnds 1-4 dc (4 rnds)
Rnd 5 (dc2, dc2 into next st) twice (8)
Rnds 6-7 dc (2 rnds)
Rnd 8 (dc2, dc2tog) twice (6)
Lightly stuff toe and continue
Rnd 9 (dc1, dc2tog) twice (4)
Break yarn.

Lightly stuff thigh and sew flat across top to close.

WINGS

Please don't wade too deep into the categorising of these wings. I am not an ornithologist and some of these flapping birds can fly and some of the soaring birds merely hover. Enjoy the fact that you can multi task while whipping up these standard forms (especially once you get onto your fifth or sixth pair).

TIP

Before sewing wings with colour changing in place, manipulate the colour change jog in or out on the right and left wings respectively to hide this on the inside when sewn into place.

1    **2**    **3** 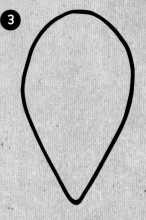   **4**

1 FLYING WINGS (make two)

Begin by dc6 into ring
Rnd 1 (dc1, dc2 into next st) 3 times (9)
Rnd 2 dc8, dc2 into next st (10)
Rnd 3 dc
Rnd 4 dc9, dc2 into next st (11)
Rnd 5 dc
Rnd 6 dc10, dc2 into next st (12)
Rnd 7 dc
Rnd 8 dc11, dc2 into next st (13)
Rnd 9 dc
Rnd 10 dc12, dc2 into next st (14)
Rnd 11 dc
Rnd 12 (dc6, dc2 into next st) twice (16)
Rnd 13 dc2 into next st, dc14, dc2 into next st (18)
Rnd 14 dc2 into next st, dc16, dc2 into next st (20)
Rnd 15 dc2 into next st, dc18, dc2 into next st (22)
Rnd 16 dc2 into next st, dc20, dc2 into next st (24)
Rnd 17 dc2 into next st, dc22, dc2 into next st (26)
Rnds 18-21 dc (4 rnds)
Rnd 22 (dc11, dc2tog) twice (24)
Rnd 23 (dc2, dc2tog) 6 times (18)
Rnd 24 dc
Rnd 25 (dc1, dc2tog) 6 times (12)
Rnd 26 (dc2tog) 6 times (6)
Break yarn, gather stitches. Do not stuff.

2 SOARING WINGS (make two)

Begin by dc6 into ring
Rnd 1 (dc1, dc2 into next st) 3 times (9)
Rnd 2 dc8, dc2 into next st (10)
Rnd 3 dc9, dc2 into next st (11)
Rnd 4 dc10, dc2 into next st (12)
Rnd 5 dc11, dc2 into next st (13)
Rnd 6 dc12, dc2 into next st (14)
Rnd 7 dc13, dc2 into next st (15)
Rnd 8 dc14, dc2 into next st (16)
Rnd 9 dc15, dc2 into next st (17)
Rnd 10 dc16, dc2 into next st (18)
Rnd 11 dc17, dc2 into next st (19)
Rnd 12 dc18, dc2 into next st (20)
Rnd 13 dc19, dc2 into next st (21)
Rnd 14 dc20, dc2 into next st (22)
Rnd 15 dc21, dc2 into next st (23)
Rnd 16 dc22, dc2 into next st (24)
Rnd 17 dc2 into next st, dc22, dc2 into next st (26)
Rnd 18 dc2 into next st, dc24, dc2 into next st (28)
Rnd 19 dc27, dc2 into next st (29)
Rnd 20 dc28, dc2 into next st (30)
Rnd 21 (dc3, dc2tog) 6 times (24)
Rnd 22 (dc2tog) 12 times (12)
Rnd 23 (dc2tog) 6 times (6)
Break yarn, gather stitches. Do not stuff.

3 FLAPPING WINGS (make two)

Begin by dc6 into ring
Rnd 1 (dc2 into next st) 6 times (12)
Rnd 2 (dc1, dc2 into next st) 6 times (18)
Rnd 3 (dc2, dc2 into next st) 6 times (24)
Rnds 4-5 dc (2 rnds)
Rnd 6 (dc2, dc2tog) 6 times (18)
Rnds 7-8 dc (2 rnds)
Rnd 9 (dc4, dc2tog) 3 times (15)
Rnd 10 dc
Rnd 11 (dc1, dc2tog) 5 times (10)
Rnds 12-13 dc (2 rnds)
Rnd 14 (dc2tog) 5 times (5)
Break yarn, gather stitches. Do not stuff.

4 ORNAMENTAL WINGS (make two)

Begin by dc5 into ring
Rnd 1 (dc2 into next st) 5 times (10)
Rnd 2 (dc1, dc2 into next st) 5 times (15)
Rnd 3 dc
Rnd 4 (dc3, dc2tog) 3 times (12)
Rnd 5 dc
Rnd 6 (dc2, dc2tog) 3 times (9)
Rnd 7 (dc1, dc2tog) 3 times (6)
Rnd 8 (dc2tog) 3 times (3)
Break yarn, gather stitches. Do not stuff.

LEVEL 1

The birds in Level 1 require knowledge of only the basics of crochet, including very simple colour changing. Cut your yarn after the change. You don't need to worry about sewing in the ends; just leave them inside the part. These birds are suitable for beginners who have read the *Technicals* section.

A few of the birds in this section will use the PERCHING leg and have a 'back toe' that is added on at the end. Omitting this is the perfect solution for a beginner to be able to successfully complete their first project using one of these patterns without worrying about too many new techniques at once. For the twitchers and perfectionists amongst you, tackle the SLIP STITCH TRAVERSE technique. It sounds much more intimidating than it is and gives a perfect finish to the foot.

ERNEST the Canary

DAVE the Gull

DUKE the Mallard

CELINE the Dove

SOPHIA the Flamingo

VINCE the Blue-Footed Booby

DORA the Wood Pigeon

INA the Stork

DESMOND the Blue Tit

ALAN the Magpie

BARNEY the Barn Owl

HUCK the Pelican

ETHEL the Kiwi

JACOB the Hoopoe

ERNEST
the Canary

Ernest is one of the best health and safety inspectors in the business. Report writing, investigating and measuring all manner of noise levels, height restrictions and vibrations is his thing. He takes the responsibility for protecting everyone around him very seriously (much to the annoyance of his three sons who sometimes sneak out to the park without their helmets on, to hit each other with sticks). Luckily for them, and all of his friends, co-workers and wife, he has a favourite and very distinctive tune, which he whistles while going about his work, so it's quite easy to quickly cease whatever seemingly dangerous activity you're up to and get your feathers straight in time.

YARN REQUIRED

50g TOFT DK yarn Yellow
25g TOFT DK yarn Oatmeal

See also *You Will Need* and *Size Options*.

BODY/NECK/HEAD

Work as standard in Yellow

LEGS (make two)

Working in Yellow

Ch12 and sl st to join into a circle

Rnds 1-5 dc (5 rnds)
Rnd 6 (dc2, dc2tog) 3 times (9)
Rnd 7 (dc1, dc2tog) 3 times (6)

Change to Oatmeal

Rnds 8-11 dc (4 rnds)
Rnd 12 (dc2 into next st) 6 times (12)
Rnds 13-14 dc (2 rnds)
Rnd 15 (dc2tog) 6 times (6)
Rnds 16-18 dc (3 rnds)
Rnd 19 (dc2 into next st) 6 times (12)
Rnd 20 (dc1, dc2 into next st) 6 times (18)

Split into three rnds of 6 sts and work each as follows:

Rnds 1-3 dc (3 rnds)
Rnd 4 dc2tog, dc4 (5)
Rnds 5-6 dc (2 rnds)
Rnd 7 dc2tog, dc3 (4)

Break yarn.

BACK TOE

Working in Oatmeal

SLIP STITCH TRAVERSE a 6-st ring on back of foot and work as follows:

Rnd 1 dc
Rnd 2 dc2tog, dc4 (5)
Rnds 3-4 dc (2 rnds)
Rnd 5 dc2tog, dc3 (4)

Break yarn.

Lightly stuff thigh and sew flat across top to close.

WINGS (make two)

Working in Yellow

Begin by dc6 into ring

Rnd 1 (dc1, dc2 into next st) 3 times (9)
Rnd 2 dc8, dc2 into next st (10)
Rnd 3 dc
Rnd 4 dc9, dc2 into next st (11)
Rnd 5 dc
Rnd 6 dc10, dc2 into next st (12)
Rnd 7 dc
Rnd 8 dc11, dc2 into next st (13)
Rnd 9 dc
Rnd 10 dc12, dc2 into next st (14)
Rnd 11 dc
Rnd 12 (dc6, dc2 into next st) twice (16)
Rnd 13 dc2 into next st, dc14, dc2 into next st (18)
Rnd 14 dc2 into next st, dc16, dc2 into next st (20)
Rnd 15 dc2 into next st, dc18, dc2 into next st (22)
Rnd 16 dc2 into next st, dc20, dc2 into next st (24)
Rnd 17 dc2 into next st, dc22, dc2 into next st (26)
Rnds 18-21 dc (4 rnds)
Rnd 22 (dc11, dc2tog) twice (24)
Rnd 23 (dc2, dc2tog) 6 times (18)
Rnd 24 dc
Rnd 25 (dc1, dc2tog) 6 times (12)
Rnd 26 (dc2tog) 6 times (6)

Break yarn, gather stitches. Do not stuff.

BEAK

Working in Oatmeal

Ch15 and sl st to join into a circle

Rnd 1 dc
Rnd 2 (dc3, dc2tog) 3 times (12)
Rnd 3 (dc2, dc2tog) 3 times (9)
Rnd 4 dc
Rnd 5 (dc1, dc2tog) 3 times (6)

Stuff lightly and sew into position.

TAIL

Working in Yellow

Ch16 and sl st to join into a circle

Rnds 1-6 dc (6 rnds)

Split into two rnds of 8 sts and work each as follows:

Rnds 1-4 dc (4 rnds)
Rnd 5 dc7, dc2 into next st (9)
Rnds 6-8 dc (3 rnds)
Rnd 9 dc8, dc2 into next st (10)
Rnds 10-12 dc (3 rnds)
Rnd 13 (dc3, dc2tog) twice (8)
Rnd 14 (dc2, dc2tog) twice (6)
Rnd 15 (dc2tog) 3 times (3)

Break yarn.

Do not stuff. Sew flat across top to close.

Finish by sewing eyes into place with Black yarn.

DAVE
the Gull

Dave has an opportunistic philosophy and a nomadic lifestyle as he's yet to find someone to build a sandcastle for and make an egg with. For breakfast he likes to search the seafront dustbins for any trace of yesterday's forgotten picnic, but to sate his lunchtime appetite he needs to resort to more desperate measures. His favourite food is any kind of potato. When hunger calls he's not afraid to start dive-bombing for fresh salt and vinegary chips straight out of the sandy hands of unwitting children.

YARN REQUIRED

25g TOFT DK yarn Cream
25g TOFT DK yarn Yellow
25g TOFT DK yarn Shale

See also *You Will Need* and *Size Options*.

BODY/NECK/HEAD

Work as standard in Cream

LEGS (make two)

Work as standard PADDLING starting in Cream and changing to Yellow after Rnd 7

WINGS (make two)

Work as standard SOARING in Shale

BEAK

Working in Yellow

Ch12 and sl st to join into a circle

Rnds 1-5 dc (5 rnds)

Rnd 6 (dc4, dc2tog) twice (10)

Rnds 7-8 dc (2 rnds)

Rnd 9 (dc2 into next st) twice, dc8 (12)

Rnds 10-11 dc (2 rnds)

Rnd 12 (dc2tog) 3 times, dc6 (9)

Rnd 13 (dc2tog) 3 times, dc3 (6)

Rnd 14 dc

Rnd 15 (dc2tog) 3 times (3)

Stuff lightly and sew into position.

TAIL

Working in Cream

Ch16 and sl st to join into a circle

Change to Shale

Rnds 1-6 dc (6 rnds)

Split into two rnds of 8 sts and work each as follows:

Rnds 1-4 dc (4 rnds)

Rnd 5 dc7, dc2 into next st (9)

Rnds 6-8 dc (3 rnds)

Rnd 9 dc8, dc2 into next st (10)

Rnds 10-12 dc (3 rnds)

Rnd 13 (dc3, dc2tog) twice (8)

Rnd 14 (dc2, dc2tog) twice (6)

Rnd 15 (dc2tog) 3 times (3)

Break yarn.

Do not stuff. Sew flat across top to close.

Finish by sewing eyes into place with Black yarn.

DUKE
the Mallard

Duke is a duck about town. He is a wild but distinctly urban drake with a slicked-back wet-look comb-over and brightly coloured trousers. Despite his caddish looks he's never short of a new duck to fall for his classic good looks and is always to be found waddling round his local city's parks with his latest sweetheart on his wing. He will read her mediocre love-poetry while they patiently wait for everyone's children to go home, so they can take their turn on the merry-go-round. Then he'll treat her to an ice-cream, and wait for the sun to go down to make his move.

YARN REQUIRED

25g TOFT DK yarn Silver
25g TOFT DK yarn Orange
25g TOFT DK yarn Green
25g TOFT DK yarn Yellow
25g TOFT DK yarn Charcoal
25g TOFT DK yarn Chestnut
25g TOFT DK yarn Cream

See also *You Will Need* and *Size Options*.

BODY/NECK/HEAD

Work as standard in Silver until after Rnd 19 and then continue:

Change to Chestnut

Rnd 20 (dc3, dc2tog) 6 times (24)

Rnd 21 dc

Change to Cream

Rnd 22 dc3, (dc2tog) 9 times, dc3 (15)

Change to Green

Rnd 23 dc3, (dc2tog) 5 times, dc2 (10)

Rnd 24 dc

Rnd 25 (dc2 into next st) 10 times (20)

Rnd 26 (dc3, dc2 into next st) 5 times (25)

Rnd 27 (dc4, dc2 into next st) 5 times (30)

Rnd 28 (dc2, dc2 into next st) 10 times (40)

Rnds 29-31 dc (3 rnds)

Rnd 32 (dc8, dc2tog) 4 times (36)

Rnd 33 dc

Rnd 34 (dc4, dc2tog) 6 times (30)

Rnd 35 (dc3, dc2tog) 6 times (24)

Rnd 36 (dc2, dc2tog) 6 times (18)

Rnd 37 dc

Rnd 38 (dc2tog) 9 times (9)

Stuff and gather remaining stitches to close.

LEGS (make two)

Work as standard PADDLING starting in Silver and changing to Orange after Rnd 7

Lightly stuff thigh and foot and sew flat across top to close.

WINGS (make two)

Work as standard FLYING in Silver

BEAK

Working in Yellow

Begin by dc6 into ring

Rnd 1 (dc2 into next st) 6 times (12)

Rnd 2 (dc1, dc2 into next st) 6 times (18)

Rnds 3-8 dc (6 rnds)

Rnd 9 (dc7, dc2tog) twice (16)

Rnd 10 dc

Rnd 11 (dc7, dc2 into next st) twice (18)

Rnd 12 dc

Rnd 13 (dc5, dc2 into next st) 3 times (21)

Stuff lightly and sew into position.

TAIL

Working in Silver

Ch12 and sl st to join into a circle

Change to Charcoal

Rnds 1-4 dc (4 rnds)

Rnd 5 (dc4, dc2tog) twice (10)

Rnds 6-9 dc (4 rnds)

Rnd 10 (dc3, dc2tog) twice (8)

Rnds 11-12 dc (2 rnds)

Rnd 13 (dc2tog) 4 times (4)

Break yarn.

Do not stuff. Sew flat across top to close.

Sew the tail into usual position and then sew a length of yarn upwards from the base through the tip and pull tight before securing to make the shape curl upwards towards the body.

Finish by sewing eyes into place with Black yarn.

CELINE
the Dove

Celine is an artist who lives in her own perfectly balanced regime; it takes a severe dose of order and discipline to balance her explosive expressions of colour. If you ever have the pleasure of meeting her you'll be soothed and calmed by her immaculate and tranquil demeanour, but once she's cooped up in her studio she creates chaos, disorder and discordant mess on her canvases. When she's not to be found channelling peace, conciliation and tranquillity (or splashing and mixing paint) she'll be knee-deep in peroxide reinstating her perfection; it's a tough job maintaining the purest shade of white.

YARN REQUIRED

75g TOFT DK yarn Cream
25g TOFT DK yarn Peony

See also *You Will Need* and *Size Options*.

BODY/NECK/HEAD

Work as standard in Cream

LEGS (make two)

Work as standard PERCHING in Cream changing to Peony after Rnd 5 working TIBIA and TARSUS as Rnds 1-3 dc (3 rnds)

WINGS (make two)

Work as standard FLYING in Cream

BEAK

Working in Peony
Ch8 and sl st to join into a circle
Rnds 1-2 dc (2 rnds)
Rnd 3 (dc2, dc2tog) twice (6)
Rnds 4-5 dc (2 rnds)
Rnd 6 (dc2tog) 3 times (3)
Do not stuff. Fold flat and sew into position.

LOWER TAIL

Working in Cream
Ch18 and sl st to join into a circle
Rnd 1 dc
Rnd 2 (dc2, dc2 into next st) 6 times (24)
Rnd 3 dc
Split into three rnds of 8 sts and work each as follows:
Rnds 1-3 dc (3 rnds)
Rnd 4 (dc3, dc2 into next st) twice (10)
Rnds 5-12 dc (8 rnds)
Rnd 13 (dc2tog) 5 times (5)
Break yarn.
Do not stuff. Sew flat across top to close.

UPPER TAIL

Working in Cream
Ch12 and sl st to join into a circle
Rnd 1 dc
Rnd 2 (dc2, dc2 into next st) 4 times (16)
Split into two rnds of 8 sts and work each as follows:
Rnds 1-2 dc (2 rnds)
Rnd 3 (dc3, dc2 into next st) twice (10)
Rnds 4-9 dc (6 rnds)
Rnd 10 (dc2tog) 5 times (5)
Break yarn.
Do not stuff. Sew flat across top to close.

Sew both tail pieces into position with the two-pronged piece above the three-pronged piece.

Finish by sewing eyes into place with Black yarn.

SOPHIA
the Flamingo

Sophia has not quite grown into her legs yet. This week at school she has had a few tough days when the smaller birds pointed out her knobbly knees, so she's developed a bit of a habit of standing on one leg. Her friends say that the other girls are just jealous, and that picking on Sophia's height distracts from their own worries about their small wings. After a good chat with her mum Sophia drifts off to sleep reassured that one day soon she'll tower over all the other birds with an elegance and femininity befitting her colour.

YARN REQUIRED

75g TOFT DK yarn Pink
25g TOFT DK yarn Cream
25g TOFT DK yarn Charcoal

See also *You Will Need* and *Size Options*.

BODY/NECK/HEAD

Work as standard in Pink working NECK as Rnds 1-6 dc (6 rnds)

LEGS (make two)

Working in Pink

Ch15 and sl st to join into a circle

Rnds 1-2 dc (2 rnds)

Rnd 3 (dc3, dc2tog) 3 times (12)

Rnd 4 (dc2, dc2tog) 3 times (9)

Rnds 5-6 dc (2 rnds)

Rnd 7 (dc1, dc2tog) 3 times (6)

Rnds 8-18 dc (11 rnds)

Rnd 19 (dc2 into next st) 6 times (12)

Rnds 20-21 dc (2 rnds)

Rnd 22 (dc2tog) 6 times (6)

Rnds 23-33 dc (11 rnds)

Rnd 34 (dc2 into next st) 6 times (12)

Rnd 35 dc

Rnd 36 (dc5, dc2 into next st) twice (14)

Rnd 37 (dc6, dc2 into next st) twice (16)

Rnd 38 (dc7, dc2 into next st) twice (18)

Rnds 39-43 dc (5 rnds)

Working in Charcoal split into three rnds of 6 sts and work each as follows:

Rnd 1 dc

Rnd 2 (dc2tog) 3 times (3)

Break yarn.

Lightly stuff thigh and sew flat across top to close.

WINGS (make two)

Work as standard FLYING in Charcoal changing to Pink after Rnd 8

BEAK

Working in Cream

Ch18 and sl st to join into a circle

Rnds 1-4 dc (4 rnds)

Rnd 5 (dc4, dc2tog) 3 times (15)

Rnds 6-8 dc (3 rnds)

Change to Charcoal

Rnd 9 (dc2 into next st) 5 times, (dc2tog) 5 times (15)

Rnds 10-11 dc (2 rnds)

Rnd 12 (dc2tog) 6 times, dc3 (9)

Rnd 13 (dc2tog) 3 times, dc3 (6)

Rnd 14 dc

Rnd 15 (dc2tog) 3 times (3)

Stuff lightly and sew into position.

TAIL

Working in Pink

Ch18 and sl st to join into a circle

Rnds 1-3 dc (3 rnds)

Rnd 4 (dc2, dc2 into next st) 6 times (24)

Rnd 5 dc

Split into three rnds of 8 sts and work each as follows:

Rnds 1-7 dc (7 rnds)

Rnd 8 (dc2, dc2tog) twice (6)

Rnd 9 (dc2tog) 3 times (3)

Break yarn.

Do not stuff. Sew flat across top to close.

Finish by sewing eyes into place with Black yarn.

VINCE
the Blue-Footed Booby

Vince is a bird who struts to his own tune and his garish taste in clothing makes him stand out from the hatch. He fancies himself as a gift to the glittery revolving dance floor, and his strong cologne and fluorescent outfits ensure the hens all know he's there. Pride of place in his nest is a three-foot mirror ball, which he ensures is always dust-free and glinting in the sunlight. It makes for quite a vigorous cleaning routine, but that and his hundreds of other shiny, perfectly polished surfaces, mean he's never short of a chance to admire how he shakes his tail feathers.

YARN REQUIRED

25g TOFT DK yarn Cream
25g TOFT DK yarn Turquoise
25g TOFT DK yarn Chestnut
25g TOFT DK yarn Shale

See also *You Will Need* and *Size Options*.

BODY/NECK/HEAD

Work as standard in Cream working NECK as Rnds 1-3 dc (3 rnds)

LEGS (make two)

Working in Cream

Ch16 and sl st to join into a circle

Rnds 1-2 dc (2 rnds)

Rnd 3 (dc2, dc2tog) 4 times (12)

Rnd 4 (dc1, dc2tog) 4 times (8)

Then change to Turquoise and continue to work as standard SWIMMING starting with TIBIA

WINGS (make two)

Working as standard FLYING in Chestnut

BEAK

Working in Shale

Ch20 and sl st to join into a circle

Rnd 1 dc

Rnd 2 (dc8, dc2tog) twice (18)

Rnd 3 dc

Rnd 4 (dc1, dc2tog) 6 times (12)

Rnd 5 (dc1, dc2tog) 4 times (8)

Rnds 6-13 dc (8 rnds)

Rnd 14 (dc2tog) 4 times (4)

Stuff lightly and sew into position.

EYES (make two)

Working in Shale

Begin by dc6 into ring

Sew into position on either side of beak.

TAIL

Working in Cream

Ch16 and sl st to join into a circle

Change to Chestnut

Rnds 1-6 dc (6 rnds)

Split into two rnds of 8 sts and work each as follows:

Rnds 1-4 dc (4 rnds)

Rnd 5 dc7, dc2 into next st (9)

Rnds 6-8 dc (3 rnds)

Rnd 9 dc8, dc2 into next st (10)

Rnds 10-12 dc (3 rnds)

Rnd 13 (dc3, dc2tog) twice (8)

Rnd 14 (dc2, dc2tog) twice (6)

Rnd 15 (dc2tog) 3 times (3)

Break yarn.

Do not stuff. Sew flat across top to close.

Finish by sewing eyes into place with Black yarn.

DORA
the Wood Pigeon

Dora is a loveable and very friendly bird with a habit of falling asleep at inappropriate times throughout the day. Think of her whenever you receive a call from a suspiciously unknown number, and especially one that when you answer there's no one there. Chances are Dora could be quietly snoring into her head-set at the other end of the line. You got off lightly if you caught her on a snooze, because when she's awake she has the most persuasive coo around and you'd have probably found you'd bought extra roof insurance you didn't know you even needed, before you got a chance to hang up.

YARN REQUIRED

50g TOFT DK yarn Shale
25g TOFT DK yarn Silver
25g TOFT DK yarn Violet
25g TOFT DK yarn Oatmeal
25g TOFT DK yarn Cream

See also *You Will Need* and *Size Options*.

BODY/NECK/HEAD

Work as standard in Silver changing to Violet after Rnd 10 and to Shale after NECK

LEGS (make two)

Work as standard PERCHING in Silver changing to Oatmeal after Rnd 5 working TIBIA and TARSUS as Rnds 1-3 dc (3 rnds)

WINGS (make two)

Work as standard FLYING in Shale

BEAK

Working in Oatmeal
Ch8 and sl st to join into a circle
Rnds 1-2 dc (2 rnds)
Rnd 3 (dc2, dc2tog) twice (6)
Rnds 4-5 dc (2 rnds)
Rnd 6 (dc2tog) 3 times (3)
Do not stuff.

PATCHES (make two)

Working in Cream
Begin by dc6 into ring
Rnd 1 (dc1, dc2 into next st) 3 times (9)
Rnd 2 (dc2, dc2 into next st) 3 times (12)
Sew into position on either side of head.

TAIL

Working in Silver
Ch16 and sl st to join into a circle
Change to Shale
Rnds 1-6 dc (6 rnds)
Split into two rnds of 8 sts and work each as follows:
Rnds 1-4 dc (4 rnds)
Rnd 5 dc7, dc2 into next st (9)
Rnds 6-8 dc (3 rnds)
Rnd 9 dc8, dc2 into next st (10)
Rnds 10-12 dc (3 rnds)
Rnd 13 (dc3, dc2tog) twice (8)
Rnd 14 (dc2, dc2tog) twice (6)
Rnd 15 (dc2tog) 3 times (3)
Break yarn.
Do not stuff. Sew flat across top to close.

Finish by sewing eyes into place with Black yarn.

INA
the Stork

Ina is a midwife who loves new life, tiny feet and the joy that motherhood brings to all the birds she meets. Rather than exhausted, she finds she clocks off her twelve-hour shifts exhilarated by her work, and this means that she has had the energy to sample many of the world's most weird and wonderful hobbies over the last twenty years. Despite discovering that she really is very good at fencing, figurine painting and calligraphy (to name but a few) she's settled upon joining her local choir. All things considered, this is an odd choice for a leggy mute bird, so perhaps there's some truth in one little sparrow's stories about her and the handsome choir conductor.

YARN REQUIRED

50g TOFT DK yarn Cream
25g TOFT DK yarn Orange
25g TOFT DK yarn Charcoal

See also *You Will Need* and *Size Options*.

BODY/NECK/HEAD

Work as standard in Cream working NECK as Rnds 1-6 dc (6 rnds)

LEGS (make two)

Working in Cream

Ch12 and sl st to join into a circle

Rnds 1-3 dc (3 rnds)

Rnd 4 (dc2, dc2tog) 3 times (9)

Rnd 5 (dc1, dc2tog) 3 times (6)

Change to Orange

Rnds 6-14 dc (9 rnds)

Rnd 15 (dc2 into next st) 6 times (12)

Rnds 16-17 dc (2 rnds)

Rnd 18 (dc2tog) 6 times (6)

Rnds 19-28 dc (10 rnds)

Rnd 29 (dc2 into next st) 6 times (12)

Rnd 30 (dc1, dc2 into next st) 6 times (18)

Split into three rnds of 6 sts and work each as follows:

Rnds 1-4 dc (4 rnds)

Rnd 5 dc2tog, dc4 (5)

Rnds 6-7 dc (2 rnds)

Rnd 8 dc2tog, dc3 (4)

Rnd 9 (dc2tog) twice (2)

Break yarn.

Lightly stuff thigh and sew flat across top to close.

BACK TOE

Working in Orange

SLIP STITCH TRAVERSE a 6-st ring on back of foot and work as follows:

Rnds 1-2 dc (2 rnds)

Rnd 3 (dc2tog) 3 times (3)

Break yarn.

WINGS (make two)

Work as standard FLYING in Charcoal changing to Cream after Rnd 8

BEAK

Working in Orange

Ch15 and sl st to join into a circle

Rnds 1-3 dc (3 rnds)

Rnd 4 (dc3, dc2tog) 3 times (12)

Rnds 5-7 dc (3 rnds)

Rnd 8 (dc2, dc2tog) 3 times (9)

Rnds 9-11 dc (3 rnds)

Rnd 12 (dc1, dc2tog) 3 times (6)

Rnds 13-14 dc (2 rnds)

Rnd 15 (dc2tog) 3 times (3)

Stuff lightly and sew into position.

TAIL

Working in Cream

Ch18 and sl st to join into a circle

Rnds 1-3 dc (3 rnds)

Rnd 4 (dc2, dc2 into next st) 6 times (24)

Rnd 5 dc

Split into three rnds of 8 sts and work each as follows:

Rnds 1-3 dc (3 rnds)

Change to Charcoal

Rnds 4-7 dc (4 rnds)

Rnd 8 (dc2, dc2tog) twice (6)

Rnd 9 (dc2tog) 3 times (3)

Break yarn.

Do not stuff. Sew flat across top to close.

Finish by sewing eyes into place with Black yarn.

DESMOND
the Blue Tit

Desmond is the most twitchy of twitchers (although he takes great offense to the term). You see Desmond isn't just in the bird-watching game to tick a rare bird off his list, he takes careful and lengthy notes on every single bird he sees. Even if it's just a common garden bird, his notebook is out, perfectly sharpened pencil at the ready, and he settles in to discreetly observe what others might never have noticed before. With his gilet loaded up with enamel pin badges from every nature reserve that has ever made one, this bird watcher always has his binoculars around his neck and a flask of hot milky tea or two in the boot of his car.

YARN REQUIRED

25g TOFT DK yarn Yellow
25g TOFT DK yarn Blue
25g TOFT DK yarn Shale
25g TOFT DK yarn Cream
25g TOFT DK yarn Charcoal

See also *You Will Need* and *Size Options*.

BODY/NECK/HEAD

Work as standard in Yellow until after Rnd 21 and then continue:

Change to Charcoal

Rnd 22 dc3, (dc2tog) 9 times, dc3 (15)

Rnd 23 dc3, (dc2tog) 5 times, dc2 (10)

Change to Cream

Rnd 24 dc

Rnd 25 (dc2 into next st) 10 times (20)

Rnd 26 (dc3, dc2 into next st) 5 times (25)

Rnd 27 (dc4, dc2 into next st) 5 times (30)

Rnd 28 (dc2, dc2 into next st) 10 times (40)

Rnd 29 dc

Change to Charcoal

Rnds 30-31 dc (2 rnds)

Change to Cream

Rnd 32 (dc8, dc2tog) 4 times (36)

Rnd 33 dc

Rnd 34 (dc4, dc2tog) 6 times (30)

Change to Blue

Rnd 35 (dc3, dc2tog) 6 times (24)

Rnd 36 (dc2, dc2tog) 6 times (18)

Rnd 37 dc

Rnd 38 (dc2tog) 9 times (9)

Stuff and gather remaining stitches to close.

LEGS (make two)

Work as standard PERCHING in Yellow changing to Shale after Rnd 5 working TIBIA as Rnds 1-3 (3 rnds) and TARSUS as Rnds 1-4 dc (4 rnds)

WINGS (make two)

Working as standard FLYING in Blue changing to Cream after Rnd 13 and Blue after Rnd 16

BEAK

Working in Shale
Ch8 and sl st to join into a circle

Rnd 1 dc2tog, dc6 (7)

Rnd 2 dc2tog, dc5 (6)

Rnd 3 dc2tog, dc4 (5)

Rnd 4 dc2tog, dc3 (4)

Do not stuff. Sew into position.

TAIL

Working in Yellow
Ch18 and sl st to join into a circle

Change to Blue

Rnds 1-3 dc (3 rnds)

Rnd 4 (dc2, dc2 into next st) 6 times (24)

Rnd 5 dc

Split into three rnds of 8 sts and work each as follows:

Rnds 1-7 dc (7 rnds)

Rnd 8 (dc2, dc2tog) twice (6)

Rnd 9 (dc2tog) 3 times (3)

Break yarn.

Do not stuff. Sew flat across top to close.

Working in Charcoal embroider between the beak and the neck.

Finish by sewing eyes into place with Black yarn.

ALAN
the Magpie

Alan is just moving into his golden years and is unsure about adopting a pace of existence with time to reflect. He managed successfully to steer an acclaimed career and a happy family unit through all the sorrows and joys that life throws at you. With his daughter's new-born girl and boy to keep things busy, he might not feel the drop in pace for a while. Although lamenting the move into retirement, it frees him up for some big adventures: more time to discover the secret places in the world he's always been too busy to stop and explore.

YARN REQUIRED

25g TOFT DK yarn Cream
25g TOFT DK yarn Charcoal
25g TOFT DK yarn Steel
25g TOFT DK yarn Kale

See also *You Will Need* and *Size Options*.

BODY/NECK/HEAD

Work as standard in Cream changing to Charcoal after Rnd 14

LEGS (make two)

Working in Charcoal

Ch12 and sl st to join into a circle

Rnds 1-6 dc (6 rnds)

Rnd 7 (dc2, dc2tog) 3 times (9)

Rnd 8 (dc1, dc2tog) 3 times (6)

Change to Steel and continue to work as standard PERCHING starting with TIBIA as Rnds 1-4 dc (4 rnds) and working TARSUS as Rnds 1-4 dc (4 rnds)

WINGS (make two)

Work as standard FLYING in Kale changing to Cream after Rnd 15

BEAK

Working in Steel

Ch18 and sl st to join into a circle

Rnds 1-4 dc (4 rnds)

Rnd 5 (dc4, dc2tog) 3 times (15)

Rnds 6-8 dc (3 rnds)

Rnd 9 (dc3, dc2tog) 3 times (12)

Rnds 10-11 dc (2 rnds)

Rnd 12 (dc2, dc2tog) 3 times (9)

Rnds 13-14 dc (2 rnds)

Rnd 15 (dc1, dc2tog) 3 times (6)

Stuff lightly and sew into position.

TAIL

Working in Charcoal

Ch16 and sl st to join into a circle

Change to Kale

Rnds 1-6 dc (6 rnds)

Split into two rnds of 8 sts rnds and work each as follows:

Rnds 1-4 dc (4 rnds)

Rnd 5 dc7, dc2 into next st (9)

Rnds 6-8 dc (3 rnds)

Rnd 9 dc8, dc2 into next st (10)

Rnds 10-12 dc (3 rnds)

Rnd 13 (dc3, dc2tog) twice (8)

Rnd 14 (dc2, dc2tog) twice (6)

Rnd 15 (dc2tog) 3 times (3)

Break yarn.

Do not stuff. Sew flat across top to close.

Finish by sewing eyes into place with Black yarn.

BARNEY
the Barn Owl

Barney is a number-crunching love-sick owl; a mathematics teacher whose mum is desperately trying her best to mend his broken heart. Lately the look in his shiny mischievous eyes has been replaced with a wide-eyed vacant stare, and as each day goes by he gets a little bit paler and not even his mum's home-cooking can fix it. Until he once again meets that night-loving individual to laugh at him while he calculates the exact angle at which to hunt prey, you can hear his wistful screeching in the last few hours before dawn.

YARN REQUIRED

50g TOFT DK yarn Camel
25g TOFT DK yarn Cream
25g TOFT DK yarn Silver

See also *You Will Need* and *Size Options*.

BODY/NECK/HEAD

Work as standard in Cream changing to Camel after NECK

LEGS (make two)

Working in Cream

Ch12 and sl st to join into a circle

Rnd 1 dc

Rnd 2 (dc2, dc2tog) 3 times (9)

Rnds 3-8 dc (6 rnds)

Rnd 9 dc7, dc2tog (8)

Rnds 10-13 dc (4 rnds)

Change to Camel

Rnd 14 (dc2 into next st) 8 times (16)

Rnd 15 (dc7, dc2 into next st) twice (18)

Split into three rnds of 6 sts and work each as follows:

Rnds 1-4 dc (4 rnds)

Rnd 5 dc5, dc2 into next st (7)

Rnd 6 dc

Rnd 7 dc6, dc2 into next st (8)

Rnd 8 dc

Rnd 9 (dc2tog) 4 times (4)

Change to Silver

Rnd 10 dc

Rnd 11 (dc2tog) twice (2)

Break yarn.

Lightly stuff thigh and sew flat across top to close.

BACK TOE

Working in Camel

SLIP STITCH TRAVERSE a 6-st ring on back of foot and work as follows:

Rnds 1-3 dc (3 rnds)

Rnd 4 (dc1, dc2tog) twice (4)

Change to Silver

Rnd 5 dc

Rnd 6 (dc2tog) twice (2)

Break yarn.

WINGS (make two)

Work as standard SOARING in Camel

Complete by embroidering stitches across the wings in Silver.

EYE PATCHES (make two)

Working in Cream

Begin by dc6 into ring

Rnd 1 (dc2 into next st) 6 times (12)

Rnd 2 (dc1, dc2 into next st) 6 times (18)

Rnd 3 dc9 Camel (incomplete rnd)

Sew into position on face meeting in the middle.

BEAK

Working in Silver

Sl st into position between the eye patches, ch5 and dc4 back down chain, sl st into head

Use the ends to sew the beak flat.

TAIL

Working in Cream

Ch16 and sl st to join into a circle

Rnds 1-2 dc (2 rnds)

Rnd 3 (dc1, dc2 into next st) 8 times (24)

Rnds 4-5 dc (2 rnds)

Change to Camel

Split into three rnds of 8 sts and work right and left 8-st rnds as follows:

Rnds 1-4 dc (4 rnds)

Rnd 5 dc7, dc2 into next st (9)

Rnd 6 dc

Rnd 7 dc8, dc2 into next st (10)

Rnds 8-10 dc (3 rnds)

Rnd 11 (dc3, dc2tog) twice (8)

Rnd 12 (dc2, dc2tog) twice (6)

Rnd 13 (dc2tog) 3 times (3)

Break yarn.

Rejoin in Camel and work central 8-st rnd as follows:

Rnds 1-4 dc (4 rnds)

Rnd 5 dc7, dc2 into next st (9)

Rnds 6-9 dc (4 rnds)

Rnd 10 dc8, dc2 into next st (10)

Rnd 11-13 dc (3 rnds)

Rnd 14 (dc3, dc2tog) twice (8)

Rnd 15 (dc2, dc2tog) twice (6)

Rnd 16 (dc2tog) 3 times (3)

Break yarn.

Do not stuff. Sew flat across top to close.

Finish by sewing eyes into place with Black yarn.

HUCK
the Pelican

Huck is a fire-fighting hero. In between pole-sliding drills, and of course responding to any actual emergencies, he's become a demon poker player, enthusiastic baker and has a ping-pong back hand that you really wouldn't want to get in the way of. Contrary to what his well-worn apron, drawer of utensils and recipe book collection would suggest, he's actually a very average cook. Rather than lack of skill or effort however, this may just be because, generally halfway though the most vital process in any meal, he's called away to save the day and scoop up more kittens in his beak.

YARN REQUIRED

50g TOFT DK yarn Cream
25g TOFT DK yarn Yellow
25g TOFT DK yarn Charcoal

See also *You Will Need* and *Size Options*.

BODY/NECK/HEAD

Work as standard in Cream working NECK as Rnds 1-5 dc (5 rnds)

LEGS (make two)

Work as standard SWIMMING in Cream changing to Yellow after Rnd 7

WINGS (make two)

Work as standard SOARING in Charcoal changing to Cream after Rnd 12

BEAK

Working in Yellow

Begin by dc6 into ring

Rnd 1 (dc2 into next st) 6 times (12)

Rnd 2 (dc1, dc2 into next st) 6 times (18)

Rnd 3 (dc2, dc2 into next st) 6 times (24)

Rnds 4-8 dc (5 rnds)

Rnd 9 (dc2 into next st, dc1) 4 times (incomplete rnd)

Count 10 sts backwards, split into a rnd and work as follows:

Rnds 1-10 dc (10 rnds)

Rnd 11 (dc3, dc2tog) twice (8)

Rnds 12-14 dc (3 rnds)

Rnd 15 (dc2, dc2tog) twice (6)

Stuff the bottom section lightly, then fold the long 10-st rnd down and sew together to close.

Sew into position.

TAIL

Working in Cream

Ch18 and sl st to join into a circle

Rnds 1-2 dc (2 rnds)

Rnd 3 (dc2, dc2 into next st) 6 times (24)

Rnd 4 dc

Split into three rnds of 8 sts and work each as follows:

Rnds 1-4 dc (4 rnds)

Rnd 5 (dc2tog) 4 times (4)

Break yarn.

Do not stuff. Sew flat across top to close.

Finish by sewing eyes into place with Black yarn.

ETHEL
the Kiwi

Ethel has been happily married for thirty years this year. In her time as the perfectly dedicated wife she's worked hard to build up her reputation as the hen that lays the biggest eggs of them all. Her success as a mother she puts down to her time spent honing her phenomenal sense of smell. She follows her beak on what to eat and what to not eat, filling up on only the finest and most nutritious super-seeds she can find until she's overstuffed and fit to burst. Then once she's laid her egg, she defers all responsibility to her dutiful husband, puts her feet up and waits for hatching time.

YARN REQUIRED

50g TOFT DK yarn Fudge
25g TOFT DK yarn Stone

See also *You Will Need* and *Size Options*.

BODY/NECK/HEAD

Work as standard in Fudge

LEGS (make two)

Working in Fudge

Ch12 and sl st to join into a circle

Rnds 1-3 dc (3 rnds)

Rnd 4 (dc2, dc2tog) 3 times (9)

Rnd 5 (dc1, dc2tog) 3 times (6)

Change to Stone

Rnds 6-10 dc (5 rnds)

Rnd 11 (dc2 into next st) 6 times (12)

Rnds 12-13 dc (2 rnds)

Rnd 14 (dc2tog) 6 times (6)

Rnds 15-19 dc (5 rnds)

Rnd 20 (dc2 into next st) 6 times (12)

Rnd 21 (dc1, dc2 into next st) 6 times (18)

Split into three rnds of 6 sts and work each as follows:

Rnds 1-3 dc (3 rnds)

Rnd 4 dc2tog, dc4 (5)

Rnds 5-6 dc (2 rnds)

Rnd 7 dc2tog, dc3 (4)

Break yarn.

Lightly stuff thigh and sew flat across top to close.

WINGS (make two)

Working in Fudge

Begin by dc5 into ring

Rnd 1 (dc2 into next st) 5 times (10)

Rnd 2 (dc1, dc2 into next st) 5 times (15)

Rnd 3 dc

Rnd 4 (dc3, dc2tog) 3 times (12)

Rnd 5 dc

Rnd 6 (dc2, dc2tog) 3 times (9)

Rnd 7 (dc1, dc2tog) 3 times (6)

Rnd 8 (dc2tog) 3 times (3)

Break yarn, gather stitches. Do not stuff.

BEAK

Working in Stone

Ch18 and sl st to join into a circle

Rnds 1-4 dc (4 rnds)

Rnd 5 (dc4, dc2tog) 3 times (15)

Rnd 6 dc

Rnd 7 (dc2tog) 3 times, dc9 (12)

Rnd 8 dc

Rnd 9 dc10, dc2tog (11)

Rnd 10 dc9, dc2tog (10)

Rnd 11 dc8, dc2tog (9)

Rnds 12-13 dc (2 rnds)

Rnd 14 dc7, dc2tog (8)

Rnd 15 (dc2, dc2tog) twice (6)

Rnds 16-19 dc (4 rnds)

Rnd 20 (dc1, dc2tog) twice (4)

Rnd 21 (dc2tog) twice (2)

Stuff firmly and sew into position.

FEATHERS

Working in Fudge

Work ch12 CHAIN LOOPS all over the body and head (leave the bottom of the body plain to ensure balance when sitting).

Finish by sewing eyes and nostrils into place with Black yarn.

JACOB
the Hoopoe

Jacob has the brilliant kind of mind that leaves half the people he meets utterly confused and the other half awestruck by his genius. Misunderstood by many, this bird can see the world in a totally different way to others, finding beauty in the ugly, rhythm in the chaos and inspiration almost everywhere. In a bid to find a way to be able to express his vision he is working through every craft he can until he finds 'his thing'. Currently he identifies as an embroidery-loving sewist who can knit, but then the next textile adventure is only ever around the next corner!

YARN REQUIRED

50g TOFT DK yarn Coral
25g TOFT DK yarn Steel
25g TOFT DK yarn Charcoal
25g TOFT DK yarn Cream

See also *You Will Need* and *Size Options*.

BODY/NECK/HEAD

Work as standard in Coral

LEGS (make two)

Work as standard PERCHING in Coral changing to Steel after Rnd 5 working TIBIA as Rnds 1-7 dc (7 rnds) and TARSUS as Rnds 1-8 dc (8 rnds)

WINGS (make two)

Starting in Charcoal work as standard FLYING working 2 rnds Charcoal, 2 rnds Cream (dc6 into ring counts as first round)

BEAK

Working in Steel
Ch11 and sl st to join into a circle
Rnd 1 dc
Rnd 2 dc9, dc2tog (10)
Rnd 3 dc8, dc2tog (9)
Rnds 4-6 dc (3 rnds)
Rnd 7 dc7, dc2tog (8)
Rnds 8-9 dc (2 rnds)
Rnd 10 dc6, dc2tog (7)
Rnd 11 dc5, dc2tog (6)
Rnd 12 dc4, dc2tog (5)
Rnd 13 dc3, dc2tog (4)
Stuff lightly and sew into position.

CREST

Working in Coral
Ch30 and sl st to join into a circle
Rnds 1-2 dc (2 rnds)
Split into five rnds of 6 sts and work each as follows:
Rnds 1-8 dc (8 rnds)
Change to Charcoal
Rnd 9 (dc1, dc2 into next st) 3 times (9)
Rnd 10 dc
Rnd 11 (dc1, dc2tog) 3 times (6)
Break yarn.
Stuff lightly and sew into position on head.

TAIL

Working in Coral
Ch16 and sl st to join into a circle
Continue working 2 rnds Charcoal and 2 rnds Cream throughout
Rnds 1-6 dc (6 rnds)
Split into two rnds of 8 sts and work each as follows:
Rnds 1-4 dc (4 rnds)
Rnd 5 dc7, dc2 into next st (9)
Rnds 6-8 dc (3 rnds)
Rnd 9 dc8, dc2 into next st (10)
Rnds 10-12 dc (3 rnds)
Rnd 13 (dc3, dc2tog) twice (8)
Rnd 14 (dc2, dc2tog) twice (6)
Rnd 15 (dc2tog) 3 times (3)
Break yarn.
Do not stuff. Sew flat across top to close.

Finish by sewing eyes into place with Black yarn.

LEVEL 2

Level 2 birds introduce patterns that use extra stitches such as the half-treble and treble. You will also master making a bobble and then move on to the fluffy feathers created using the LOOP STITCH technique towards the end of this section. Loop stitches can be left as loops or cut once completed to create a different texture on the bird.

HENRY the Raven

RORY the Northern Cardinal

MARGOT the Swan

HAZEL the Hen

ARTHUR the Blue-Winged Teal

ORLANDO the Roseate Spoonbill

PEDRO the Wine-Throated Hummingbird

ROSS the Turkey

ELIZABETH the Dodo

FLORIAN the Ostrich

EMILY the Vulture

DUDLEY the Red Grouse

ZANE the Grey Crowned Crane

ABRAHAM the Bald Eagle

KEVIN the Cassowary

TRAVIS the Pink Robin

TRICIA the Silkie Chicken

HENRY
the Raven

Henry has been endowed with a strut, stature and presence from a bygone era. He has had the privilege of the best education money can buy and now he's applying his intelligence and training to serving his country. He knows his self-assured, purposeful stride will only get stronger as his pride and confidence grow with age and direction, and now he's ready to prove himself. As a chick he dreamt of a tall wall in the middle of nowhere defending good from evil, but he's now ready to accept the reality of what a soldier's life offers him.

YARN REQUIRED

50g TOFT DK yarn Charcoal
25g TOFT DK yarn Steel

See also *You Will Need* and *Size Options*.

BODY/NECK/HEAD

Work as standard in Charcoal

LEGS (make two)

Working in Charcoal

Ch12 and sl st to join into a circle

Rnds 1-6 dc (6 rnds)

Rnd 7 (dc2, dc2tog) 3 times (9)

Rnd 8 (dc1, dc2tog) 3 times (6)

Change to Steel and continue to work as standard PERCHING starting with TIBIA as Rnds 1-3 dc (3 rnds) and working TARSUS as 1-4 dc (4 rnds)

WINGS (make two)

Work as standard FLYING in Charcoal

BEAK

Working in Steel

Ch18 and sl st to join into a circle

Rnds 1-4 dc (4 rnds)

Rnd 5 (dc4, dc2tog) 3 times (15)

Rnds 6-8 dc (3 rnds)

Rnd 9 (dc3, dc2tog) 3 times (12)

Rnds 10-11 dc (2 rnds)

Rnd 12 (dc2, dc2tog) 3 times (9)

Rnds 13-14 dc (2 rnds)

Rnd 15 (dc1, dc2tog) 3 times (6)

Stuff lightly and sew into position.

COLLAR

Working in Charcoal

Sl st into position on head two rnds up from NECK and work feathers around the head as follows:

(ch10 and sl st 3, dc3, htr3 back down chain, sl st into head) 9 times

Break yarn.

TAIL

Working in Charcoal

Ch16 and sl st to join into a circle

Rnds 1-6 dc (6 rnds)

Split into two rnds of 8 sts and work each as follows:

Rnds 1-4 dc (4 rnds)

Rnd 5 dc7, dc2 into next st (9)

Rnds 6-8 dc (3 rnds)

Rnd 9 dc8, dc2 into next st (10)

Rnds 10-12 dc (3 rnds)

Rnd 13 (dc3, dc2tog) twice (8)

Rnd 14 (dc2, dc2tog) twice (6)

Rnd 15 (dc2tog) 3 times (3)

Break yarn.

Do not stuff. Sew flat across top to close.

Finish by sewing eyes into place with Black yarn.

RORY
the Northern Cardinal

Rory was a Christmas tree farmer before he could even fly, lovingly nurturing his family's potted tree from one year to the next. What this Christmas-loving little bird doesn't know about keeping a tree in your house for a month of the year is frankly not worth knowing. 'What kind of tree would you like this year Madam? Spruce? Like your needles on the floor do you?' After decades spent growing firs, pines and spruces of every variety Rory now solely farms balsam firs. Upright branches loaded with soft needles and that essential 'spicy' Christmas scent, he is never more at home than in those perfectly spaced rows of deep green forest.

YARN REQUIRED

50g TOFT DK yarn Ruby
25g TOFT DK yarn Stone
25g TOFT DK yarn Charcoal

See also *You Will Need* and *Size Options*.

BODY/NECK/HEAD

Work as standard in Ruby until after Rnd 21 and then continue:

Rnd 22 (dc2tog) 9 times, dc6 (15)

Rnd 23 (dc2tog) 5 times, dc5 (10)

Stuff and continue

Rnd 24 dc

Rnd 25 (dc2 into next st) 10 times (20)

Rnd 26 (dc3, dc2 into next st) 5 times (25)

Rnd 27 (dc4, dc2 into next st) 5 times (30)

Rnd 28 (dc2, dc2 into next st) 10 times (40)

Rnds 29-31 dc (3 rnds)

Rnd 32 (dc8, dc2tog) 4 times (36)

Rnd 33 dc

Rnd 34 (dc4, dc2tog) 6 times (30)

Rnd 35 (dc3, dc2tog) 6 times (24)

Rnd 36 (dc2, dc2tog) 6 times (18)

Rnds 37-38 dc (2 rnds)

Rnd 39 (dc2tog) 5 times, dc8 (13)

Rnds 40-41 dc (2 rnds)

Rnd 42 dc2, dc2tog, dc9 (12)

Rnd 43 dc2tog, dc1, dc2tog, dc7 (10)

Rnd 44 (dc2tog) 3 times, dc4 (7)

Stuff and gather remaining stitches to close.

LEGS (make two)

Work as standard PERCHING in Ruby changing to Stone after Rnd 5

WINGS (make two)

Work as standard FLYING in Charcoal changing to Ruby after Rnd 6

MASK

Working in Charcoal

Ch11 and work in rows as follows:

Rows 1-10 turn, dc10 (10 rows)

Fasten off and sew into position on front of face (with rows horizontal across the rnds).

BEAK

Working in Charcoal

Ch15 and sl st to join into a circle

Change to Ruby

Rnd 1 dc

Rnd 2 (dc3, dc2tog) 3 times (12)

Rnd 3 (dc2, dc2tog) 3 times (9)

Rnd 4 dc

Rnd 5 (dc1, dc2tog) 3 times (6)

Stuff lightly and sew into position on top of mask.

TAIL

Working in Ruby

Ch16 and sl st to join into a circle

Rnds 1-6 dc (6 rnds)

Split into two rnds of 8 sts and work each as follows:

Rnds 1-4 dc (4 rnds)

Rnd 5 dc7, dc2 into next st (9)

Rnds 6-8 dc (3 rnds)

Rnd 9 dc8, dc2 into next st (10)

Rnds 10-12 dc (3 rnds)

Rnd 13 (dc4, dc2 into next st) twice (12)

Rnds 14-16 dc (3 rnds)

Rnd 17 (dc2tog) 6 times (6)

Break yarn.

Do not stuff. Sew flat across top to close.

Finish by sewing eyes into place with Black yarn.

WORKING ROWS

1. Chain the number of stitches stated in the pattern.

2. Starting in the second chain from hook, work back along these chain stitches to create the first row.

3. Turn piece so that the back of the previous row is facing you. Start in the first stitch next to your hook and work the next row along the row of stitches.

MARGOT
the Swan

Margot the swan is one of those unforgettable ladies that all young women should meet. With an ethereal sense of her own style that instantly makes everyone else look scruffy, dated and unoriginal, Margot exudes a quality that, if you get close to her, you know might make what happens next change your mind about everything. If you take her fancy she may well stop to speak to you, often with a perfect one-liner of wit, or a question that works on fifteen levels, followed by a swoop of the chin and a piercing snatch of eye contact. As you fluster around for a response she turns and moves on, and leaves you feeling awkward and confused but oddly reassured that you were the one she chose to encounter.

YARN REQUIRED

50g TOFT DK yarn Cream
25g TOFT DK yarn Charcoal
25g TOFT DK yarn Orange

See also *You Will Need* and *Size Options*.

BODY/NECK/HEAD

Work as standard in Cream working NECK as Rnds 1-6 dc (6 rnds)

LEGS (make two)

Work as standard PADDLING in Cream changing to Charcoal after Rnd 7

WINGS (make two)

Working in Cream

Begin by dc6 into ring

Rnd 1 (dc2 into next st) 6 times (12)

Rnd 2 (dc1, dc2 into next st) 6 times (18)

Rnd 3 (dc2, dc2 into next st) 6 times (24)

Rnd 4 (dc3, dc2 into next st) 6 times (30)

Rnds 5-10 dc (6 rnds)

Count 10 sts backwards, split and work these sts as follows:

Rnds 1-4 dc (4 rnds)

Rnd 5 (dc2tog) 5 times (5)

Break yarn.

Rejoin and work remaining 20 sts as follows:

Rnds 1-3 dc (3 rnds)

Rnd 4 dc5 (incomplete rnd)

Split into two rnds of 10 sts and work first rnd as follows:

Rnds 1-4 dc (4 rnds)

Rnd 5 (dc2tog) 5 times (5)

Break yarn.

Rejoin and work final 10-st rnd as follows:

Rnds 1-6 dc (6 rnds)

Rnd 7 (dc2tog) 5 times (5)

Break yarn.

Do not stuff.

BEAK

Working in Charcoal

Begin by dc6 into ring

Change to Orange

Rnd 1 (dc2 into next st) 6 times (12)

Rnd 2 (dc1, dc2 into next st) 6 times (18)

Rnds 3-5 dc (3 rnds)

Rnd 6 (dc4, dc2tog) 3 times (15)

Rnds 7-12 dc (6 rnds)

Rnd 13 (dc4, dc2 into next st) 3 times (18)

Rnd 14 dc

Change to Charcoal

Rnd 15 dc

Rnd 16 (dc2, dc2 into next st) 6 times (24)

Stuff lightly and sew into position.

TAIL

Working in Cream

Ch18 and sl st to join into a circle

Rnd 1 dc

Rnd 2 (dc2, dc2 into next st) 6 times (24)

Rnd 3 (dc5, dc2 into next st) 4 times (28)

Split into three rnds with one rnd of 12 sts in the middle and two rnds of 8 sts either side

Work each 8-st rnd as follows:

Rnds 1-2 dc (2 rnds)

Rnd 3 (dc2tog) 4 times (4)

Break yarn.

Rejoin and work the central 12-st rnd as follows:

Rnds 1-4 dc (4 rnds)

Rnd 5 (dc2, dc2tog) 3 times (9)

Rnd 6 (dc1, dc2tog) 3 times (6)

Rnd 7 (dc2tog) 3 times (3)

Break yarn.

Do not stuff. Sew flat across top to close.

Finish by sewing eyes into place with Black yarn.

HAZEL
the Hen

Hazel is a frantically industrious red hen. Long since done asking for help from anyone, she's enrolled in every night class going in order to learn to do, well, almost everything. Forget finding someone to assist you in removing some wallpaper, this independent and highly practical hen can change tyres, lay brick walls and has even baked and frosted a five-tier wedding cake. And not only that, she does the lot without the assistance of machines; seriously, this hen won't even take help from her plug-in whisk! After she's sown the corn, harvested and made the flour, the pleasure is in eating a mouthful of her 100 percent fabulous bread.

YARN REQUIRED

50g TOFT DK yarn Fudge
25g TOFT DK yarn Oatmeal
25g TOFT DK yarn Orange

See also *You Will Need* and *Size Options*.

BODY/NECK/HEAD

Work as standard in Fudge

LEGS (make two)

Work as standard PERCHING in Fudge changing to Oatmeal after Rnd 5 working TIBIA as Rnd 1 dc and TARSUS as Rnds 1-8 dc (8 rnds)

WINGS (make two)

Work as standard FLAPPING in Fudge

COMB

Working in Orange

Ch18 and sl st to join into a circle

Rnd 1 dc

Rnd 2 (dc2, dc2 into next st) 6 times (24)

Split into three rnds of 8 sts and work each as follows:

Rnd 1 dc

Rnd 2 (dc2, dc2tog) twice (6)

Rnd 3 dc

Rnd 4 (dc2tog) 3 times (3)

Break yarn.

Stuff lightly and sew into position on head.

MASK

Working in Orange

Begin by dc6 into ring

Rnd 1 (dc2 into next st) 6 times (12)

Rnd 2 (dc2 into next st) 12 times (24)

Rnd 3 (dc2 into next st) 24 times (48)

Sew into position on head beneath comb.

WATTLE (make two)

Working in Orange

Begin by dc6 into ring

Rnd 1 (dc1, dc2 into next st) 3 times (9)

Rnds 2-3 dc (2 rnds)

Rnd 4 (dc1, dc2tog) 3 times (6)

Rnd 5 dc

Sew into position beneath mask.

BEAK

Working in Oatmeal

Ch8 and sl st to join into a circle

Rnds 1-2 dc (2 rnds)

Rnd 3 (dc2, dc2tog) twice (6)

Rnds 4-5 dc (2 rnds)

Rnd 6 (dc1, dc2tog) twice (4)

Stuff lightly and sew into position on top of mask.

TAIL

Working in Fudge

Sl st into body at one side of usual tail position and work 5 FEATHERS in a row followed by two rows of 3 FEATHERS as follows:

FEATHERS

Ch12 and miss 2, tr10 back down chain, sl st into body.

Finish by sewing eyes into place with Black yarn.

ARTHUR
the Blue-Winged Teal

Arthur is a duck of many, many words. Meet him when he's managed to have eight hours sleep and you might need to phone ahead to cancel your plans for the rest of the morning. By and large his chattering can be very interesting as he divulges everything from local gossip to national news and restaurant reviews, but there always seems to come a point when you realise that you have been watching his beak opening and closing energetically for ten minutes without a clue what's coming out of it. If that ever happens to you, offer him heart-felt thanks for the chat, enthusiastically smile, then get your head down and skuttle out of there before he starts on politics!

YARN REQUIRED

25g TOFT DK yarn Shale
25g TOFT DK yarn Chestnut
25g TOFT DK yarn Charcoal
25g TOFT DK yarn Teal
25g TOFT DK yarn Cream

See also *You Will Need* and *Size Options*.

BODY/NECK/HEAD

Work as standard in Shale working NECK as Rnds 1-5 dc (5 rnds) before changing to Chestnut and continuing with HEAD

LEGS (make two)

Work as standard PADDLING in Shale changing to Charcoal after Rnd 7

WINGS (make two)

Working in Charcoal

Begin by dc6 into ring

Rnd 1 (dc1, dc2 into next st) 3 times (9)

Rnd 2 dc8, dc2 into next st (10)

Change to Teal

Rnd 3 dc

Rnd 4 dc9, dc2 into next st (11)

Rnd 5 dc

Rnd 6 dc10, dc2 into next st (12)

Rnd 7 dc

Rnd 8 dc11, dc2 into next st (13)

Change to Shale

Rnd 9 dc

Rnd 10 dc12, dc2 into next st (14)

Rnd 11 dc

Rnd 12 (dc6, dc2 into next st) twice (16)

Rnd 13 dc2 into next st, dc14, dc2 into next st (18)

Rnd 14 dc2 into next st, dc16, dc2 into next st (20)

Rnd 15 dc2 into next st, dc18, dc2 into next st (22)

Rnd 16 dc2 into next st, dc20, dc2 into next st (24)

Rnd 17 dc2 into next st, dc22, dc2 into next st (26)

Rnds 18-19 dc (2 rnds)

Change to Cream

Rnds 20-21 dc (2 rnds)

Change to Shale

Rnd 22 (dc11, dc2tog) twice (24)

Rnd 23 (dc2, dc2tog) 6 times (18)

Rnd 24 dc

Rnd 25 (dc1, dc2tog) 6 times (12)

Rnd 26 (dc2tog) 6 times (6)

Break yarn, gather stitches. Do not stuff.

BEAK

Working in Charcoal

Begin by dc6 into ring

Rnd 1 (dc2 into next st) 6 times (12)

Rnd 2 (dc3, dc2 into next st) 3 times (15)

Rnds 3-12 dc (10 rnds)

Rnd 13 (dc4, dc2 into next st) 3 times (18)

Rnd 14 (dc5, dc2 into next st) 3 times (21)

Stuff lightly and sew into position.

MASK

Working in Teal

*Ch17 and work back down chain as follows:

Miss 2, tr9, htr3, dc3*

Work three ch5 SLIP STITCH CHAINS

Sl st into original chain and repeat from * to *.

Sew into position.

TAIL

Working in Shale

Ch24 and sl st to join into a circle

Change to Charcoal

Rnds 1-2 dc (2 rnds)

Change to Cream

Rnd 3 dc

Rnd 4 (dc6, dc2tog) 3 times (21)

Rnds 5-6 dc (2 rnds)

Rnd 7 (dc5, dc2tog) 3 times (18)

Rnd 8 dc

Rnd 9 (dc4, dc2tog) 3 times (15)

Rnd 10 (dc3, dc2tog) 3 times (12)

Rnd 11 (dc2, dc2tog) 3 times (9)

Rnd 12 (dc1, dc2tog) 3 times (6)

Break yarn.

Do not stuff. Sew flat across top to close.

Finish by sewing eyes into place with Black yarn.

ORLANDO
the Roseate Spoonbill

Orlando is a golfing pro with a superb swing and serious love for the long game. A beautiful bird, preened to perfection, and with much to be proud of glinting on his mantelpiece. When he's not enjoying a few swigs at the nineteenth hole, you'll track him down spending his winnings in one of the world's greatest spas. He'll never tire of squandering every day away from the clubhouse enjoying clay wraps, acupressure and exfoliating his aches and pains away while channelling his inner albatross.

YARN REQUIRED

50g TOFT DK yarn Cream
25g TOFT DK yarn Raspberry
25g TOFT DK yarn Pink
25g TOFT DK yarn Shale

See also *You Will Need* and *Size Options*.

BODY/NECK/HEAD

Work as standard in Cream working NECK as Rnds 1-6 dc (6 rnds)

LEGS (make two)

Working in Cream

Ch12 and sl st to join into a circle

Rnds 1-3 dc (3 rnds)

Rnd 4 (dc2, dc2tog) 3 times (9)

Rnd 5 (dc1, dc2tog) 3 times (6)

Change to Raspberry

Rnds 6-14 dc (9 rnds)

Rnd 15 (dc2 into next st) 6 times (12)

Rnds 16-17 dc (2 rnds)

Rnd 18 (dc2tog) 6 times (6)

Rnds 19-28 dc (10 rnds)

Rnd 29 (dc2 into next st) 6 times (12)

Rnd 30 (dc1, dc2 into next st) 6 times (18)

Split into three rnds of 6 sts and work each as follows:

Rnds 1-4 dc (4 rnds)

Rnd 5 dc2tog, dc4 (5)

Rnds 6-7 dc (2 rnds)

Rnd 8 dc2tog, dc3 (4)

Rnd 9 (dc2tog) twice (2)

Break yarn.

Lightly stuff thigh and sew flat across top to close.

BACK TOE

Working in Raspberry

SLIP STITCH TRAVERSE a 6-st ring on back of foot and work as follows:

Rnds 1-2 dc (2 rnds)

Rnd 3 (dc2tog) 3 times (3)

Break yarn.

WEBBING

Working in Raspberry

Sl st halfway down the inside edge of first claw, ch3 and sl st to secure halfway down the second claw, sl st into second claw one stitch below chain.

Turn and dc3 across into chain, sl st into first claw to secure, then turn and dc2 across, sl st into second claw, turn and dc1, sl st into first claw.

Repeat same technique between second and third claw.

WINGS (make two)

Work as standard FLYING in Pink changing to Raspberry after Rnd 17 and Cream after Rnd 21

BEAK

Working in Shale

Begin by dc6 into ring

Rnd 1 (dc2 into next st) 6 times (12)

Rnd 2 (dc1, dc2 into next st) 6 times (18)

Rnd 3 (dc2, dc2 into next st) 6 times (24)

Rnds 4-8 dc (5 rnds)

Rnd 9 (dc2, dc2tog) 6 times (18)

Rnd 10 dc

Rnd 11 (dc1, dc2tog) 6 times (12)

Rnd 12-17 dc (6 rnds)

Rnd 18 (dc1, dc2 into next st) 6 times (18)

Rnd 19-21 dc (3 rnds)

Stuff end lightly and sew flat across top to close.

TAIL

Working in Cream

Ch18 and sl st to join into a circle

Change to Pink

Rnds 1-3 dc (3 rnds)

Rnd 4 (dc2, dc2 into next st) 6 times (24)

Rnd 5 dc

Split into three rnds of 8 sts and work each as follows:

Rnds 1-7 dc (7 rnds)

Rnd 8 (dc2, dc2tog) twice (6)

Rnd 9 (dc2tog) 3 times (3)

Break yarn.

Do not stuff. Sew flat across top to close.

Finish by sewing eyes into place with Black yarn.

PEDRO
the Wine-Throated Hummingbird

Prior to the pandemic, Pedro was the kind of bird who alternated between beans on toast and noodles for dinner each night. Finding himself with far more time on his hands than he knew what to do with, he began consuming days worth of cooking TV, and before he knew it was attempting to flambé his mid-afternoon snack. Some people spent their time in lockdown getting fit, mastering a language or building an extension on the house; this bird has worked his culinary palate and skills right up from a student to a master chef.

YARN REQUIRED

25g TOFT DK yarn Cream
25g TOFT DK yarn Mushroom
25g TOFT DK yarn Green
25g TOFT DK yarn Camel
25g TOFT DK yarn Magenta

See also *You Will Need* and *Size Options*.

BODY/NECK/HEAD

Work as standard in Cream changing to Mushroom after Rnd 23 and Green after HEAD Rnd 9

LEGS (make two)

Work as standard PERCHING in Cream changing to Mushroom after Rnd 5 working TIBIA as Rnds 1-3 dc (3 rnds) dc and TARSUS as Rnds 1-4 dc (4 rnds)

WINGS (make two)

Work as standard FLYING in Camel changing to Green after Rnd 4

BEAK

Working in Mushroom
Ch10 and sl st to join into a circle
Rnds 1-6 dc (6 rnds)
Rnd 7 dc2tog, dc8 (9)
Rnd 8 dc2tog, dc7 (8)
Rnds 9-10 dc (2 rnds)
Rnd 11 dc2tog, dc6 (7)
Rnd 12 dc2tog, dc5 (6)
Rnd 13 dc2tog, dc4 (5)
Rnd 14 dc2tog, dc3 (4)
Rnd 15 dc2tog, dc2 (3)
Stuff lightly and sew into position.

TAIL

Working in Cream
Ch18 and sl st to join into a circle
Change to Camel
Rnds 1-3 dc (3 rnds)
Rnd 4 (dc2, dc2 into next st) 6 times (24)
Rnd 5 dc
Split into three rnds of 8 sts and work each as follows:
Rnds 1-6 dc (6 rnds)
Change to Mushroom
Rnds 7-8 dc (2 rnds)
Rnd 9 (dc1, dc2 into next st) 4 times (12)
Rnd 10 (dc2, dc2tog) 3 times (9)
Change to Cream
Rnd 11 (dc1, dc2tog) 3 times (6)
Rnd 12 (dc2tog) 3 times (3)
Break yarn.
Do not stuff. Sew flat across top to close.

GORGET

Once bird has been stuffed and sewn up
Working in Magenta
Sl st into position on head in line with bottom of beak
SLIP STITCH TRAVERSE 2 sts down head towards body
Ch6 and work back down chain as follows:
MB, sl st 2, MB, sl st 1
Break yarn and repeat 4 times more to make a row of five feathers.

Sl st into position on next rnd below
Ch9 and work back down chain as follows:
(MB, sl st 2) twice, MB, sl st 1
Break yarn and repeat 4 times more to make a row of five feathers.

Sl st into position on next rnd below
Ch12 and work back down chain as follows:
(MB, sl st 2) 3 times, MB, sl st 1
Break yarn and repeat 3 times more to make a row of four feathers.

Finish by sewing eyes into place with Black yarn.

ROSS
the Turkey

Ross is fed up with his innate ability to make everyone laugh-out-loud getting in the way of his love life. Despite several personality reinvention attempts, he just cannot seem to shed the fact that the party follows him wherever he goes, and everyone is too busy having a good time to consider a future date. Most recently he's hatched a plan to renovate his image and meet a mate by joining his local slimming group. If he can resist the temptation to gobble up everyone else's snacks then this time it might just work.

YARN REQUIRED

50g TOFT DK yarn Fudge
25g TOFT DK yarn Chestnut
25g TOFT DK yarn Stone
25g TOFT DK yarn Ruby
25g TOFT DK yarn Hyacinth
25g TOFT DK yarn Cream
25g TOFT DK yarn Charcoal

See also *You Will Need* and *Size Options.*

BODY/NECK/HEAD

Work as standard in Chestnut changing to Ruby after Rnd 23 and working NECK as Rnds 1-5 dc (5 rnds) before changing to Hyacinth and continuing with HEAD

LEGS (make two)

Work as standard PERCHING in Chestnut changing to Stone after Rnd 5 working TIBIA as Rnds 1-4 dc (4 rnds) and TARSUS as Rnds 1-5 dc (5 rnds)

WINGS (make two)

Work as standard FLAPPING in Fudge

BEAK

Working in Stone
Ch15 and sl st to join into a circle
Rnd 1 dc
Rnd 2 (dc3, dc2tog) 3 times (12)
Rnd 3 dc
Rnd 4 (dc2, dc2tog) 3 times (9)
Rnds 5-6 dc (2 rnds)
Rnd 7 (dc1, dc2tog) 3 times (6)
Rnds 8-10 dc (3 rnds)
Rnd 11 (dc2tog) twice, dc2 (4)
Stuff lightly and sew into position.

WATTLE (make two)

Working in Ruby
Begin by dc6 into ring
Ch9 and sl st 8 back down chain, (MB, sl st 2) twice around edge of ring, then (MB, sl st 2) twice, sl st 2 along chain
Break yarn and sew into position at base of neck.

SNOOD

Working in Ruby
Sl st into head at side of beak
*ch9 and work back down chain as follows:
(MB, sl st 2) twice, sl st 2
Sl st 4 over top of beak, then repeat from * once more

TAIL

Working in Fudge
Ch18 and sl st to join into a circle
Rnd 1 dc
Rnd 2 (dc2, dc2 into next st) 6 times (24)
Rnd 3 (dc3, dc2 into next st) 6 times (30)
Change to Chestnut
Rnd 4 (dc4, dc2 into next st) 6 times (36)
Change to Fudge
Rnd 5 (dc5, dc2 into next st) 6 times (42)
Rnd 6 (dc6, dc2 into next st) 6 times (48)
Split into six rnds of 8 sts and work each as follows:
Rnd 1 dc
Change to Chestnut
Rnd 2 dc
Change to Fudge
Rnds 3-5 dc (3 rnds)
Change to Chestnut
Rnd 6 (dc1, dc2 into next st) 4 times (12)
Change to Fudge
Rnds 7-9 dc (3 rnds)
Change to Charcoal
Rnd 10 dc
Change to Fudge
Rnds 11-13 dc (3 rnds)
Change to Cream
Rnd 14 (dc2tog) 6 times (6)
Break yarn.
Do not stuff. Sew flat across top to close.

Sew the tail into an upwards position on back of body.

Finish by sewing eyes into place with Black yarn.

ELIZABETH
the Dodo

There's nothing obsolete about Liz the dodo and her brilliantly organised mind. Peddling a contented happy-go-lucky attitude but remaining unobtrusively ambitious, she'll be planning distinctions not extinction into her diary. At the moment the world lies at her feet, and there's a quiet assuredness about her that says she'll get to wherever she wants to be. Sensibly she heads back to the nest nice and early most nights, combines and reprioritises her various lists, and then every morning bobs back fresh and ready to reorder the next day.

YARN REQUIRED

25g TOFT DK yarn Hyacinth
25g TOFT DK yarn Oatmeal
25g TOFT DK yarn Cream
25g TOFT DK yarn Camel

See also *You Will Need* and *Size Options*.

BODY/NECK/HEAD

Work as standard in Hyacinth

LEGS (make two)

Working in Hyacinth

Ch15 and sl st to join into a circle

Rnds 1-2 dc (2 rnds)

Rnd 3 (dc3, dc2tog) 3 times (12)

Rnds 4-5 dc (2 rnds)

Rnd 6 (dc2, dc2tog) 3 times (9)

Change to Oatmeal

Rnds 7-8 dc (2 rnds)

Rnd 9 dc7, dc2tog (8)

Rnds 10-13 dc (4 rnds)

Rnd 14 (dc2 into next st) 8 times (16)

Rnd 15 (dc7, dc2 into next st) twice (18)

Split into three rnds of 6 sts and work each as follows:

Rnds 1-4 dc (4 rnds)

Rnd 5 dc5, dc2 into next st (7)

Rnd 6 dc

Rnd 7 dc6, dc2 into next st (8)

Rnd 8 dc

Rnd 9 (dc2tog) 4 times (4)

Change to Camel

Rnd 10 dc

Rnd 11 (dc2tog) twice (2)

Break yarn.

Lightly stuff thigh and sew flat across top to close.

BACK TOE

Working in Oatmeal

SLIP STITCH TRAVERSE a 6-st ring on back of foot and work as follows:

Rnds 1-3 dc (3 rnds)

Rnd 4 (dc1, dc2tog) twice (4)

Change to Camel

Rnd 5 dc

Rnd 6 (dc2tog) twice (2)

Break yarn.

WINGS (make two)

Work as standard ORNAMENTAL in Cream

BEAK

Working in Oatmeal

Ch36 and and sl st to join into a circle

Rnd 1 dc

Rnd 2 (dc2, dc2tog) 9 times (27)

Rnd 3 (dc7, dc2tog) 3 times (24)

Rnds 4-5 dc (2 rnds)

Rnd 6 (dc2, dc2tog) 6 times (18)

Rnd 7 (dc4, dc2tog) 3 times (15)

Rnd 8 (dc3, dc2tog) 3 times (12)

Rnds 9-11 dc (3 rnds)

Rnd 12 (dc2 into next st) 6 times, dc6 (18)

Change to Camel

Rnds 13-15 dc (3 rnds)

Rnd 16 (dc2tog) 6 times, dc6 (12)

Rnd 17 (dc2tog) 5 times, dc2 (7)

Rnd 18 dc

Rnd 19 (dc2tog) 3 times, dc1 (4)

Stuff lightly and sew into position.

TAIL

Working in Cream

Work 2cm (¾in) LOOP STITCH every 4th st throughout

Begin by dc6 into ring

Rnd 1 (dc2 into next st) 6 times (12)

Rnd 2 (dc1, dc2 into next st) 6 times (18)

Rnd 3 (dc2, dc2 into next st) 6 times (24)

Rnds 4-7 dc (4 rnds)

Break yarn.

Do not stuff. Sew flat across top to close.

Finish by sewing eyes into place with Black yarn.

FLORIAN
the Ostrich

Florian works in fashion. Some say that his career path formed inside his giant egg, as from the moment of hatching he boasted a stronger beak, longer legs and more voluminous plumage than the rest of the flock had ever seen. Twenty-five years of meticulous preening has ensured he has stayed in topnotch condition (a beauty regime which adamantly rejects any 'head in the sand' treatments). Last year he astutely recognised that he had peaked in his modelling career, and is getting ready to become the pride of all who know him when he reveals his own signature collection this spring and strongly strides off the catwalk and onto the shop-floor.

YARN REQUIRED

50g TOFT DK yarn Oatmeal
25g TOFT DK yarn Charcoal
25g TOFT DK yarn Cream
25g TOFT DK yarn Stone

See also *You Will Need* and *Size Options.*

BODY/NECK/HEAD

Work as standard in Charcoal changing to Oatmeal after Rnd 22 with NECK as Rnds 1-10 dc (10 rnds)

LEGS (make two)

Working in Charcoal
Ch16 and sl st to join into a circle
Change to Oatmeal
Rnds 1-5 dc (5 rnds)
Rnd 6 (dc2, dc2tog) 4 times (12)
Rnd 7 (dc2, dc2tog) 3 times (9)
Rnds 8-13 dc (6 rnds)
Rnd 14 (dc2, dc2 into next st) 3 times (12)
Rnds 15-16 dc (2 rnds)
Rnd 17 (dc1, dc2tog) 4 times (8)
Rnds 18-27 dc (10 rnds)
Rnd 28 (dc1, dc2 into next st) 4 times (12)
Split into two rnds of 6 sts and work each as follows:
Rnds 1-3 dc (3 rnds)
Rnd 4 (dc1, dc2 into next st) 3 times (9)
Rnds 5-8 dc (4 rnds)
Rnd 9 (dc1, dc2tog) 3 times (6)
Rnd 10 dc
Change to Charcoal
Rnd 11 dc
Rnd 12 (dc2tog) 3 times (3)
Break yarn.
Lightly stuff thigh and sew flat across top to close.

WINGS (make two)

Working in Charcoal
Begin by dc6 into ring
Rnd 1 (dc2 into next st) 6 times (12)
Rnd 2 (dc1, dc2 into next st) 6 times (18)
Rnd 3 (dc2, dc2 into next st) 6 times (24)
Rnd 4 (dc3, dc2 into next st) 6 times (30)
Rnds 5-6 dc (2 rnds)
Rnd 7 (dc3, dc2tog) 6 times (24)
Change to Cream
Count 8 sts backwards, split and work these sts as follows:
Rnds 1-4 dc (4 rnds)
Rnd 5 (dc2tog) 4 times (4)
Break yarn.

Rejoin in Charcoal and work remaining 16 sts as follows:
Rnds 1-3 dc (3 rnds)
Change to Cream
Split into two rnds of 8 sts and work first rnd as follows:
Rnds 1-4 dc (4 rnds)
Rnd 5 (dc2tog) 4 times (4)
Break yarn.

Rejoin in Charcoal and work last 8-st rnd as follows:
Rnds 1-2 dc (2 rnds)
Change to Cream
Rnds 1-4 dc (4 rnds)
Rnd 5 (dc2tog) 4 times (4)
Break yarn.
Do not stuff.

BEAK

Working in Stone
Begin by dc6 into ring
Rnd 1 (dc2 into next st) 6 times (12)
Rnds 2-7 dc (6 rnds)
Rnd 8 (dc1, dc2 into next st) 3 times, dc6 (15)
Rnd 9 (dc2 into next st, dc2) 3 times, dc6 (18)
Rnd 10 dc
Stuff lightly and sew into position.

TAIL

Working in Cream
Work 2cm (¾in) LOOP STITCH every other st throughout
Begin by dc6 into ring
Rnd 1 (dc2 into next st) 6 times (12)
Rnd 2 (dc1, dc2 into next st) 6 times (18)
Rnd 3 (dc2, dc2 into next st) 6 times (24)
Rnds 4-7 dc (4 rnds)
Break yarn.
Do not stuff. Sew flat across top to close.

Finish by sewing eyes into place with Black yarn.

EMILY
the Vulture

Emily is not your average young vulture and should not be judged by her hump. Far from a scavenging, unscrupulous loiterer, she is a fast-paced risk-taker who really likes to get things done. Having recently flown the nest, perhaps a little later than some, she's enjoying independent decision making, from how to budget her bills to which leftovers to pack into her lunchbox. Every morning she flies off to her new job with a wave of enthusiasm that keeps her perhaps a little above the speed limit, and lands her ready to tear into the latest day.

YARN REQUIRED

50g TOFT DK yarn Charcoal
25g TOFT DK yarn Peony
25g TOFT DK yarn Cream
25g TOFT DK yarn Silver

See also *You Will Need* and *Size Options*.

BODY/NECK/HEAD

Work as standard in Charcoal changing to Cream after Rnd 23 working NECK as Rnds 1-4 dc (4 rnds) with 2cm (¾in) LOOP STITCH every stitch then change to Peony and work HEAD

LEGS (make two)

Working in Cream

Ch15 and sl st to join into a circle

Continue working 2cm (¾in) LOOP STITCH every st

Rnds 1-2 dc (2 rnds)

Rnd 3 (dc3, dc2tog) 3 times (12)

Rnds 4-5 dc (2 rnds)

Rnd 6 (dc2, dc2tog) 3 times (9)

Change to Silver and continue without loops

Rnds 7-12 dc (6 rnds)

Rnd 13 dc7, dc2tog (8)

Rnds 14-17 dc (4 rnds)

Rnd 18 (dc2 into next st) 8 times (16)

Rnd 19 (dc7, dc2 into next st) twice (18)

Split into three rnds of 6 sts and work each as follows:

Rnds 1-4 dc (4 rnds)

Rnd 5 dc5, dc2 into next st (7)

Rnd 6 dc

Rnd 7 dc6, dc2 into next st (8)

Rnd 8 dc

Rnd 9 (dc2tog) 4 times (4)

Change to Charcoal

Rnd 10 dc

Rnd 11 (dc2tog) twice (2)

Break yarn.

BACK TOE

Working in Silver

SLIP STITCH TRAVERSE a 6-st ring on back of foot and work as follows:

Rnds 1-3 dc (3 rnds)

Rnd 4 (dc1, dc2tog) twice (4)

Change to Charcoal

Rnd 5 dc

Rnd 6 (dc2tog) twice (2)

Break yarn.

Lightly stuff thigh and sew flat across top to close.

WINGS (make two)

Work as standard SOARING in Charcoal

Sew the wings higher than usual off the top of the body either side of the neck.

BEAK

Working in Silver

Ch18 and sl st to join into a circle

Rnds 1-2 dc (2 rnds)

Rnd 3 (dc1, dc2tog) 6 times (12)

Rnd 4 dc

Rnd 5 (dc2 into next st) 6 times, dc6 (18)

Rnds 6-9 dc (4 rnds)

Change to Charcoal

Rnd 10 (dc2tog) 6 times, dc6 (12)

Rnd 11 (dc3, dc2tog) twice, dc2 (10)

Rnd 12 dc4, (dc2tog) 3 times (7)

Rnd 13 (dc2tog) twice, (dc2 into next st) twice, dc1 (7)

Stuff lightly and sew into position.

TAIL

Working in Charcoal

Ch18 and sl st to join into a circle

Rnds 1-3 dc (3 rnds)

Rnd 4 (dc2, dc2 into next st) 6 times (24)

Rnd 5 dc

Split into three rnds of 8 sts and work each as follows:

Rnds 1-7 dc (7 rnds)

Rnd 8 (dc2, dc2tog) twice (6)

Rnd 9 (dc2tog) 3 times (3)

Break yarn.

Do not stuff. Sew flat across top to close.

Finish by sewing eyes into place with Black yarn.

DUDLEY
the Red Grouse

Dudley is a lonely bird who can be found living in the East wing of a remote castle waiting for his life to start. Perhaps noble by name, but not awfully noble by nature, this soon-to-be Earl is sitting around waiting for it all to happen having not lifted a claw to anything really. Most days he spends a good few hours staring out onto the water of a loch, squinting beneath the crystal clear surface searching for something. It could be to see the fish, it could be looking for treasure, but most likely it's in hope of a frog.

YARN REQUIRED:

25g TOFT DK yarn Cocoa
25g TOFT DK yarn Chestnut
25g TOFT DK yarn Fudge
25g TOFT DK yarn Cream
25g TOFT DK yarn Oatmeal
25g TOFT DK yarn Orange

See also *You Will Need* and *Size Options*.

BODY/NECK/HEAD

Work as standard in Cocoa changing to Chestnut after Rnd 8 then Fudge after Rnd 17

LEGS (make two)

Working in Cream

Work 1cm (⅓in) LOOP STITCH every other st

Ch12 and sl st to join into a circle

Rnd 1 (dc2, dc2tog) 3 times (9)

Rnds 2-7 dc (6 rnds)

Rnd 8 dc7, dc2tog (8)

Rnds 9-10 dc (2 rnds)

Change to Oatmeal and continue without loops

Rnd 11 (dc1, dc2 into next st) 4 times (12)

Rnd 12 (dc1, dc2 into next st) 6 times (18)

Split into three rnds of 6 sts and work each as follows:

Rnds 1-3 dc (3 rnds)

Rnd 4 dc2tog, dc4 (5)

Rnds 5-6 dc (2 rnds)

Rnd 7 dc2tog, dc3 (4)

Break yarn.

BACK TOE

Working in Oatmeal

SLIP STITCH TRAVERSE a 6-st ring on back of foot and work as follows:

Rnd 1 dc

Rnd 2 dc2tog, dc4 (5)

Rnds 3-4 dc (2 rnds)

Rnd 5 dc2tog, dc3 (4)

Break yarn.

Lightly stuff thigh and sew flat across top to close.

CLAWS

Working in Cocoa

Sl st into position on the end of each toe, ch3 and sl st 1, dc1 back down chain

Break yarn and repeat on all toes and back toe.

WINGS (make two)

Work as standard FLYING in Chestnut

BEAK

Working in Oatmeal

Ch15 and sl st to join into a circle

Change to Cocoa

Rnd 1 dc

Rnd 2 (dc3, dc2tog) 3 times (12)

Rnd 3 dc2tog, dc10 (11)

Rnd 4 dc2tog, dc9 (10)

Rnd 5 (dc2tog) 5 times (5)

Rnd 6 dc2tog (incomplete rnd)

Sew flat across top to close and then sew curved into position on face.

TAIL

Working in Cocoa

Ch18 and sl st to join into a circle

Rnds 1-3 dc (3 rnds)

Rnd 4 (dc2, dc2 into next st) 6 times (24)

Rnd 5 dc

Split into three rnds of 8 sts and work each as follows:

Rnds 1-7 dc (7 rnds)

Rnd 8 (dc2, dc2tog) twice (6)

Rnd 9 (dc2tog) 3 times (3)

Break yarn.

Do not stuff. Sew flat across top to close.

Stuff and sew up your bird and then continue to add details.

Sew eyes into place with Black yarn.

EYEBROW WATTLES

Working in Orange

Sl st into position at the side of the eye and (tr2 into next st) 5 times in a curve over each eye

Break yarn and repeat over second eye.

EMBROIDERY

Work stitches onto your body and wings as follows:

Working in Fudge

Work stitches around the central Chestnut panel on the front of the body. Start the bottom row of stitches one round up from the colour change line and then stagger the placement of the stitches on the rows above.

Working in Cocoa

Work stitches in a triangle formation onto the tip of each wing.

ZANE
the Grey Crowned Crane

Having suffered a few too many jiving bridezillas stamping on his toes, Zane decided that life as a wedding photographer was not the day job he had dreamed of at art school. Swapping the chaos of confetti and cake-cutting for the tranquillity of a desert sunset was a bold move that's left this beautiful bird with plenty more time for dancing. When he's not halfway up a tree framing a landscape, you'll find him at the ballet barre perfecting a pirouette or moonwalking his way across a dance floor. With his new anti-social subject matter, life behind the lens now delivers all the time he needs to bust a move when no one is looking.

YARN REQUIRED

25g TOFT DK yarn Steel
25g TOFT DK yarn Shale
25g TOFT DK yarn Charcoal
25g TOFT DK yarn Cream
25g TOFT DK yarn Chestnut
25g TOFT DK yarn Ruby
25g TOFT DK yarn Apricot

See also *You Will Need* and *Size Options*.

BODY/NECK/HEAD

Work as standard in Steel changing to Shale after Rnd 23 with NECK as Rnds 1-8 dc (8 rnds) then change to Charcoal to continue onto HEAD changing to Cream after Rnd 2

LEGS (make two)

Work as standard PERCHING in Steel changing to Charcoal after Rnd 5 working TIBIA as Rnds 1-9 dc (9 rnds) and TARSUS as Rnds 1-10 dc (10 rnds), work FOOT and then continue:

Split into three rnds of 6 sts and work each as follows:

Rnds 1-4 dc (4 rnds)
Rnd 5 dc2tog, dc4 (5)
Rnds 6-7 dc (2 rnds)
Rnd 8 dc2tog, dc3 (4)
Rnd 9 (dc2tog) twice (2)
Break yarn.

Lightly stuff thigh and sew flat across top to close.

BACK TOE

Working in Charcoal
SLIP STITCH TRAVERSE a 6-st ring on back of foot and work as follows:

Rnds 1-2 dc (2 rnds)
Rnd 3 (dc2tog) 3 times (3)
Break yarn.

WINGS (make two)

Work as standard FLYING in Chestnut changing to Cream after Rnd 10 and Steel after Rnd 19

BEAK

Working in Shale
Ch15 and sl st to join into a circle
Rnds 1-3 dc (3 rnds)
Rnd 4 (dc3, dc2tog) 3 times (12)
Rnds 5-7 dc (3 rnds)
Rnd 8 (dc2, dc2tog) 3 times (9)
Rnds 9-11 dc (3 rnds)
Rnd 12 (dc1, dc2tog) 3 times (6)
Stuff lightly and sew into position.

HEAD PIECE

Working in Charcoal
Begin by dc6 into ring
Rnd 1 (dc2 into next st) 6 times (12)
Rnd 2 (dc1, dc2 into next st) 6 times (18)
Rnd 3 (dc2, dc2 into next st) 6 times (24)
Rnd 4 dc
Rnd 5 (dc3, dc2 into next st) 6 times (30)
Rnds 6-7 dc (2 rnds)
Rnd 8 (dc2, dc2 into next st) 4 times Charcoal, dc18 Ruby (34)
Stuff lightly and sew into position on top of head.

WATTLE

Working in Ruby
Begin by dc6 into ring
Rnd 1 (dc2 into next st) 6 times (12)
Rnds 2-3 dc (2 rnds)
Rnd 4 (dc2, dc2tog) 3 times (9)
Rnd 5 dc
Rnd 6 (dc1, dc2tog) 3 times (6)
Rnds 7-8 dc (2 rnds)
Rnd 9 (dc1, dc2 into next st) 3 times (9)
Do not stuff. Sew into position on neck.

FRONT FEATHERS

Working in Shale
Work two rows of five ch12 SLIP STITCH CHAINS at the base of the neck.

TAIL

Working in Chestnut
Ch18 and sl st to join into a circle
Rnds 1-3 dc (3 rnds)
Rnd 4 (dc2, dc2 into next st) 6 times (24)
Rnd 5 dc
Split into three rnds of 8 sts and work each as follows:
Rnds 1-7 dc (7 rnds)
Rnd 8 (dc2, dc2tog) twice (6)
Rnd 9 (dc2tog) 3 times (3)
Break yarn.
Do not stuff. Sew flat across top to close.

CROWN/TAIL DETAIL (make two)

Working in Apricot
Work 5cm (2in) LOOP STITCH every other st
Begin by dc6 into ring
Rnd 1 (dc2 into next st) 6 times (12)
Rnd 2 (dc1, dc2 into next st) 6 times (18)
Rnd 3-4 dc (2 rnds)
Rnd 5 (dc2tog) 9 times (9)
Stuff lightly and gather stitches to close.
Sew one into position at back of head where the head piece joins and the other just above the tail.

Finish by sewing eyes into place with Black yarn.

ABRAHAM
the Bald Eagle

All-American Abraham loves big cars and fishing trips. He's an optimistic hardworking bird who's everyone's best friend, and nothing upsets him more than meeting someone having a bad day. Since he graduated high school he's been steadily pursuing his lifestyle, and so far he's living the dream his mom had always hoped for him. He thinks there's nothing better than snatching an unplanned weekend away with his family, bundling the essentials into his gigantic truck and hitting the highway with a belly full of fish to look forward to.

YARN REQUIRED

50g TOFT DK yarn Chestnut
25g TOFT DK yarn Cream
25g TOFT DK yarn Yellow

See also *You Will Need* and *Size Options*.

BODY/NECK/HEAD

Work as standard in Chestnut changing to Cream after Rnd 22 and working 2cm (¾in) LOOP STITCH every stitch on Rnds 23 and NECK. Continue without loops for rest of HEAD.

LEGS (make two)

Working in Chestnut

Ch12 and sl st to join into a circle

Continue working 2cm (¾in) LOOP STITCH every other st

Rnd 1 dc

Rnd 2 (dc2, dc2tog) 3 times (9)

Rnds 3-8 dc (6 rnds)

Change to Yellow without loops

Rnd 9 dc7, dc2tog (8)

Rnds 10-13 dc (4 rnds)

Rnd 14 (dc2 into next st) 8 times (16)

Rnd 15 (dc7, dc2 into next st) twice (18)

Split into three rnds of 6 sts and work each as follows:

Rnds 1-4 dc (4 rnds)

Rnd 5 dc5, dc2 into next st (7)

Rnd 6 dc

Rnd 7 dc6, dc2 into next st (8)

Rnds 8-9 dc (2 rnds)

Rnd 10 (dc2tog) 4 times (4)

Break yarn.

Lightly stuff thigh and sew flat across top to close.

BACK TOE

Working in Yellow

SLIP STITCH TRAVERSE a 6-st ring on back of foot and work as follows:

Rnds 1-3 dc (3 rnds)

Rnd 4 (dc1, dc2tog) twice (4)

Rnd 5 dc

Break yarn.

CLAWS

Working in Chestnut

Sl st into position on the end of each toe, ch3 and sl st 1, htr1 back down chain

Break yarn and repeat on all toes and back toe.

WINGS (make two)

Work as standard SOARING in Chestnut

BEAK

Working in Yellow

Ch16 and sl st to join into a circle

Rnds 1-4 dc (4 rnds)

Rnd 5 dc4, (dc2tog) 6 times (10)

Rnd 6 (dc2 into next st) 5 times, dc5 (15)

Rnd 7 dc11, (dc2tog) twice (13)

Rnd 8 (dc2tog) twice, dc5, (dc2tog) twice (9)

Rnd 9 dc

Stuff lightly and sew tip vertically flat to create a hooked beak before sewing into position.

TAIL

Working in Chestnut

Ch18 and sl st to join into a circle

Change to Cream

Rnds 1-3 dc (3 rnds)

Rnd 4 (dc2, dc2 into next st) 6 times (24)

Rnd 5 dc

Split into three rnds of 8 sts and work each as follows:

Rnds 1-7 dc (7 rnds)

Rnd 8 (dc2, dc2tog) twice (6)

Break yarn.

Do not stuff. Sew flat across top to close.

Finish by sewing eyes into place with Black yarn.

KEVIN
the Cassowary

Kevin is a stay-at-home dad with a very full nest. Every day his wife goes out to work to do whatever it is she does (something important, something boring – he forgets), and he begins the endless housework, school run and laundry routine. Ensuring that everyone has a polished casque before leaving the house is a task in itself, but thankfully he's coached them to sprint the school run in under ten minutes so they are very rarely late. When your feet are as big as a cassowary's, four sets of muddy footprints becomes a day-long undertaking to clear up, not to mention ironing all the long socks, shorts and shirts of their incredibly sporty brood.

YARN REQUIRED

50g TOFT DK yarn Charcoal
25g TOFT DK yarn Stone
25g TOFT DK yarn Blue
25g TOFT DK yarn Orange

See also *You Will Need* and *Size Options*.

BODY/NECK/HEAD

Work as standard in Charcoal with 2cm (¾in) LOOP STITCH every 4th st changing to Orange after Rnd 23. Continue without loops working NECK as Rnds 1-3 dc (3 rnds) in Orange then change to Blue for Rnds 4-8 dc (5 rnds) before continuing with HEAD.

LEGS (make two)

Working in Charcoal

Ch21 and sl st to join into a circle

Rnds 1-4 dc (4 rnds)

Rnd 5 (dc5, dc2tog) 3 times (18)

Rnds 6-10 dc (5 rnds)

Rnd 11 (dc4, dc2tog) 3 times (15)

Change to Stone

Rnds 12-13 dc (2 rnds)

Rnd 14 (dc3, dc2tog) 3 times (12)

Rnds 15-16 dc (2 rnds)

Rnd 17 (dc2, dc2tog) 3 times (9)

Rnds 18-23 dc (6 rnds)

Rnd 24 dc7, dc2tog (8)

Rnds 25-28 dc (4 rnds)

Rnd 29 (dc2 into next st) 8 times (16)

Rnd 30 (dc7, dc2 into next st) twice (18)

Split into three rnds of 6 sts and work each as follows:

Rnds 1-4 dc (4 rnds)

Rnd 5 dc5, dc2 into next st (7)

Rnd 6 dc

Rnd 7 dc6, dc2 into next st (8)

Rnd 8 dc

Rnd 9 (dc2tog) 4 times (4)

Change to Charcoal

Rnd 10 dc

Rnd 11 (dc2tog) twice (2)

Break yarn.

Lightly stuff thigh and sew flat across top to close.

WINGS (make two)

Working in Charcoal

Work three ch16 SLIP STITCH CHAINS into position on both sides of body

BEAK

Working in Charcoal

Ch15 and sl st to join into a circle

Rnds 1-3 dc (3 rnds)

Rnd 4 (dc3, dc2tog) 3 times (12)

Rnd 5 (dc2, dc2tog) 3 times (9)

Rnds 6-8 dc (3 rnds)

Rnd 9 (dc1, dc2tog) 3 times (6)

Rnd 10 dc

Rnd 11 (dc2tog) 3 times (3)

Stuff lightly and sew into position.

TAIL

Working in Charcoal

Work 2cm (¾in) LOOP STITCH every 4th st

Begin by dc6 into ring

Rnd 1 (dc2 into next st) 6 times (12)

Rnd 2 (dc1, dc2 into next st) 6 times (18)

Rnd 3 (dc2, dc2 into next st) 6 times (24)

Rnds 4-7 dc (4 rnds)

Break yarn.

Do not stuff. Sew flat across top to close.

CASQUE

Working in Stone

Begin by dc6 into ring

Rnd 1 (dc2 into next st) 6 times (12)

Rnd 2 (dc1, dc2 into next st) 6 times (18)

Rnd 3 dc

Rnd 4 (dc2, dc2 into next st) 6 times (24)

Rnds 5-10 dc (6 rnds)

Stuff lightly and sew into position on top of head.

WATTLE (make two)

Working in Orange

Begin by dc6 into ring

Rnd 1 (dc1, dc2 into next st) 3 times (9)

Rnds 2-3 dc (2 rnds)

Rnd 4 (dc1, dc2tog) 3 times (6)

Ch4, then sl st into neck to attach.

Finish by sewing eyes into place with Black yarn.

TRAVIS
the Pink Robin

From the humble beginnings of silversmithing at his kitchen table after work, in recent years having swapped opals for emeralds, Travis has spread his wings to the city and is now one of the most famous jewellery designers in the country. This little robin first fell in love with precious stones on a school trip as a chick, heading into an opal mine wide-eyed with the beauty of these iridescent pebbles in the rock. Even now, with his days spent casting, welding and setting only the biggest and best centre stones into his designs, his favourite weekend pastime is a bit of fossicking for anything he can find.

YARN REQUIRED

50g TOFT DK yarn Sapphire
25g TOFT DK yarn Magenta
25g TOFT DK yarn Shale

See also *You Will Need* and *Size Options*.

BODY/NECK/HEAD

Work as standard in Magenta with 2cm (¾in) LOOP STITCH every other st on alternate rows changing to Sapphire after Rnd 15 and continuing without loops

LEGS (make two)

Work as standard PERCHING in Magenta changing to Shale after Rnd 5 working TIBIA as Rnds 1-3 dc (3 rnds) and TARSUS as Rnds 1-4 dc (4 rnds)

WINGS (make two)

Work as standard FLYING in Sapphire

BEAK

Working in Shale
Ch8 and sl st to join into a circle
Rnds 1-3 dc (3 rnds)
Rnd 4 dc2tog, dc6 (7)
Rnd 5 dc
Rnd 6 dc2tog, dc5 (6)
Rnd 7 (dc2tog) 3 times (3)
Do not stuff. Sew into position.

TAIL

Working in Magenta
Ch16 and sl st to join into a circle
Change to Sapphire
Rnds 1-6 dc (6 rnds)
Split into two rnds of 8 sts and work each as follows:
Rnds 1-4 dc (4 rnds)
Rnd 5 dc7, dc2 into next st (9)
Rnds 6-8 dc (3 rnds)
Rnd 9 dc8, dc2 into next st (10)
Rnds 10-12 dc (3 rnds)
Rnd 13 (dc3, dc2tog) twice (8)
Rnd 14 (dc2, dc2tog) twice (6)
Rnd 15 (dc2tog) 3 times (3)
Break yarn.
Do not stuff. Sew flat across top to close.

Cut loops and trim. Finish by sewing eyes into place with Black yarn.

TRICIA
the Silkie Chicken

Tricia is a middle-aged, self-employed aerobics instructor thrilled that so many women are still so bad at getting fit and staying thin. Her 'modern pop workout' hasn't been updated since the 80s; it worked for her and her lycra bodysuit then, and if her toy-boy and dress-size are anything to go by, then it's still working now. She's never really been seen without her mullet, sweatband and legwarmers, and if the right Madonna track comes on when she's in the supermarket, then her muscles just move on their own. She's not one for counting her eggs though, because every time the latest spinning, plating or Pilates craze takes a hold her attendance numbers take a hit as everyone heads for the next easy-fix solution to cellulite.

YARN REQUIRED

75g TOFT DK yarn Silver
25g TOFT DK yarn Steel

See also *You Will Need* and *Size Options*.

BODY/NECK/HEAD

Work as standard in Silver changing to working 3cm (1¼in) LOOP STITCH every other st after NECK

LEGS (make two)

Working in Silver with 3cm (1¼in) LOOP STITCH every other st

Ch12 and sl st to join into a circle

Rnds 1-3 dc (3 rnds)

Rnd 4 (dc2, dc2tog) 3 times (9)

Rnd 5 (dc1, dc2tog) 3 times (6)

Change to Steel without loops

Rnds 6-10 dc (5 rnds)

Rnd 11 (dc2 into next st) 6 times (12)

Rnds 12-13 dc (2 rnds)

Rnd 14 (dc2tog) 6 times (6)

Rnds 15-19 dc (5 rnds)

Change to Silver with 3cm (1¼in) LOOP STITCH every other st

Rnd 20 (dc2 into next st) 6 times (12)

Rnd 21 (dc1, dc2 into next st) 6 times (18)

Change to Steel without loops

Split into three rnds of 6 sts and work each as follows:

Rnds 1-3 dc (3 rnds)

Rnd 4 dc2tog, dc4 (5)

Rnds 5-6 dc (2 rnds)

Rnd 7 dc2tog, dc3 (4)

Break yarn.

Lightly stuff thigh and sew flat across top to close.

BACK TOE

Working in Steel

SLIP STITCH TRAVERSE a 6-st ring on back of foot and work as follows:

Rnd 1 dc

Rnd 2 dc2tog, dc4 (5)

Rnds 3-4 dc (2 rnds)

Rnd 5 dc2tog, dc3 (4)

Break yarn.

WINGS (make two)

Work as standard FLAPPING in Silver with 3cm (1¼in) LOOP STITCH every other st

BEAK

Working in Steel

Ch12 and sl st to join into a circle

Rnd 1 dc

Rnd 2 (dc4, dc2tog) twice (10)

Rnd 3 (dc3, dc2tog) twice (8)

Rnd 4 (dc2, dc2tog) twice (6)

Rnd 5 (dc2tog) twice, (dc2 into next st) twice (6)

Rnd 6 (dc2tog) twice, dc2 (4)

Stuff lightly and sew into position.

TAIL

Working in Silver

Work 3cm (1¼in) LOOP STITCH every other st

Begin by dc6 into ring

Rnd 1 (dc2 into next st) 6 times (12)

Rnd 2 (dc1, dc2 into next st) 6 times (18)

Rnd 3 (dc2, dc2 into next st) 6 times (24)

Rnds 4-7 dc (4 rnds)

Break yarn.

Do not stuff. Sew flat across top to close.

Finish by sewing eyes into place with Black yarn.

LEVEL 3

The birds in this section introduce colour changing that requires a certain level of accuracy and discipline because you will need to count a shape pattern and a colour pattern simultaneously. Should you have one more or one less stitch than you ought, or if you misplace or miscount your row starts, you will find that the colour patterns will skew and this will be hard to fix.

When working colour changes that require you to return to the original colour, run the strands behind the back of the WS, being careful not to pull the changes too tight to avoid puckering the fabric.

Always ensure you set up the change to the next colour in the last stitch of the previous instruction (see *Technicals*). The colour appears after a pattern instruction, so read to the end of a round before commencing.

ELVIS the Cockatoo

MEGHAN the Toucan

ROBIN the Robin

JORGE the Jay

GARETH the Puffin

BEN the Kingfisher

YOLANDA the Cockatiel

GIANNI the Lovebird

PUTU the Lesser Bird of Paradise

JACK the Macaw

RENÉE the Shalow's Turaco

TERENCE the Budgerigar

ENID the Long-Eared Owl

EZRA the Gouldian Finch

ROHIT the Peacock

LEVI the Red and Yellow Barbet

AGATHA the Vulturine Guinea Fowl

RAEGAN the King Penguin

CALLAHAN the Yokohama Cockerel

ELVIS
the Cockatoo

Elvis is a karaoke king with a raucous voice only his late mother loved to hear. The dawn chorus is a terrifying prospect for anyone within earshot of this squawking parrot, especially when he's pulled an all-nighter and has ignored the sundown, having bumbled from branch to branch with his renditions of the old classics. He is a late riser, letting the sun warm the stage before he hops upon it; perhaps that's the key to his longevity as some say he'll have seen a century by this time next year.

YARN REQUIRED

50g TOFT DK yarn Cream
25g TOFT DK yarn Shale
25g TOFT DK yarn Yellow

See also *You Will Need* and *Size Options*.

BODY/NECK/HEAD

Work as standard in Cream

LEGS (make two)

Work as standard CLIMBING in Cream changing to Shale after Rnd 9

WINGS (make two)

Work as standard FLYING in Cream

BEAK

Working in Shale
Ch12 and sl st to join into a circle
Rnd 1 dc
Rnd 2 (dc4, dc2tog) twice (10)
Rnd 3 (dc3, dc2tog) twice (8)
Rnd 4 (dc2, dc2tog) twice (6)
Rnd 5 (dc2tog) twice, (dc2 into next st) twice (6)
Rnd 6 (dc2tog) twice, dc2 (4)
Stuff lightly and sew into position.

CREST

Working in Yellow
Ch32 and sl st to join into a circle
Rnds 1-2 dc (2 rnds)
Split into four rnds of 8 sts and work first rnd as follows:
Rnds 1-6 dc (6 rnds)
Rnd 7 (dc2, dc2tog) twice (6)
Rnds 8-11 dc (4 rnds)
Rnd 12 (dc1, dc2tog) twice (4)
Break yarn.

Work next 8-st rnd as follows:
Rnds 1-6 dc (6 rnds)
Rnd 7 (dc2, dc2tog) twice (6)
Rnds 8-13 dc (6 rnds)
Rnd 14 (dc1, dc2tog) twice (4)
Break yarn.

Work next 8-st rnd as follows:
Rnds 1-6 dc (6 rnds)
Rnd 7 (dc2, dc2tog) twice (6)
Rnds 8-11 dc (4 rnds)
Rnd 12 (dc1, dc2tog) twice (4)
Break yarn.

Work last 8-st rnd as follows:
Rnds 1-4 dc (4 rnds)
Rnd 5 (dc2, dc2tog) twice (6)
Rnd 6 dc
Rnd 7 (dc1, dc2tog) twice (4)
Break yarn.

Stuff lightly and sew into position on top of head.

TAIL

Working in Cream
Ch18 and sl st to join into a circle
Rnds 1-3 dc (3 rnds)
Rnd 4 (dc2, dc2 into next st) 6 times (24)
Rnd 5 dc
Split into three rnds of 8 sts and work each as follows:
Rnd 1-7 dc (7 rnds)
Rnd 8 (dc2, dc2tog) twice (6)
Rnd 9 (dc2tog) 3 times (3)
Break yarn.
Do not stuff. Sew flat across top to close.

Finish by sewing eyes into place with Black yarn.

MEGHAN
the Toucan

Meghan is a little girl growing an attitude to match her beak. Like many very young women, her attention span is short for anything and everything other than princesses, fairies and the colour pink. What initially began as an interest in happy endings developed into some days when she is insistent about eating food fit only for a queen, and wearing her plastic high heels to nursery. When she's not sitting on the side of her bed, reading about a castle and kicking her feet back and forth, she can be found cruising around on her bike with her tiara on and glitzy streamers fluttering beside her from the bicycle handlebars.

YARN REQUIRED

50g TOFT DK yarn Charcoal
25g TOFT DK yarn Steel
25g TOFT DK yarn Cream
25g TOFK DK yarn Yellow
25g TOFT DK yarn Orange

See also *You Will Need* and *Size Options*.

BODY/NECK/HEAD

Work as standard in Charcoal until after Rnd 21 then continue as follows:

Rnd 22 (dc2tog) 9 times Cream, dc6 Charcoal (15)

Rnd 23 (dc2tog) 5 times Cream, dc5 Charcoal (10)

Stuff and continue

Rnd 24 dc5 Cream, dc5 Charcoal

Rnd 25 (dc2 into next st) 5 times Cream, (dc2 into next st) 5 times Charcoal (20)

Rnd 26 (dc3, dc2 into next st) twice, dc2 Cream, dc1, dc2 into next st, (dc3, dc2 into next st) twice Charcoal (25)

Rnd 27 (dc4, dc2 into next st) twice, dc2 Cream, dc2, dc2 into next st, (dc4, dc2 into next st) twice Charcoal (30)

Rnd 28 (dc2, dc2 into next st) 4 times, dc2 Cream, dc2 into next st, (dc2, dc2 into next st) 5 times Charcoal (40)

Rnds 29-31 dc18 Cream, dc22 Charcoal (3 rnds)

Rnd 32 dc8, dc2tog, dc8 Cream, dc2tog, (dc8, dc2tog) twice Charcoal (36)

Rnd 33 dc17 Cream, dc19 Charcoal

Rnd 34 (dc4, dc2tog) twice, dc4 Cream, dc2tog, (dc4, dc2tog) 3 times Charcoal (30)

Continue in Charcoal

Rnd 35 (dc3, dc2tog) 6 times (24)

Rnd 36 (dc2, dc2tog) 6 times (18)

Rnd 37 dc

Rnd 38 (dc2tog) 9 times (9)

Stuff and gather remaining stitches to close.

LEGS (make two)

Work as standard CLIMBING in Charcoal changing to Steel after Rnd 9

WINGS (make two)

Work as standard FLYING in Charcoal

BEAK

Working in Charcoal

Ch24 and sl st to join into a circle

Rnd 1 dc

Change to Yellow

Rnds 2-10 dc (9 rnds)

Rnd 11 (dc4, dc2tog) 4 times (20)

Change to Orange

Rnds 12-17 dc (6 rnds)

Rnd 18 dc16, (dc2tog) twice (18)

Rnd 19 dc

Rnd 20 dc6, (dc2tog) 3 times, dc6 (15)

Rnd 21 dc8, (dc2tog) 3 times, dc1 (12)

Change to Charcoal

Rnd 22 dc8, (dc2tog) twice (10)

Rnd 23 dc6, (dc2tog) twice (8)

Rnd 24 dc2tog, dc4, dc2tog (6)

Rnd 25 dc2tog, dc2, dc2tog (4)

Stuff lightly and sew into position.

TAIL

Working in Charcoal

Ch16 and sl st to join into a circle

Rnds 1-6 dc (6 rnds)

Split into two rnds of 8 sts and work each as follows:

Rnds 1-4 dc (4 rnds)

Rnd 5 dc7, dc2 into next st (9)

Rnds 6-8 dc (3 rnds)

Rnd 9 dc8, dc2 into next st (10)

Rnds 10-12 dc (3 rnds)

Rnd 13 (dc3, dc2tog) twice (8)

Rnd 14 (dc2, dc2tog) twice (6)

Rnd 15 (dc2tog) 3 times (3)

Break yarn.

Do not stuff. Sew flat across top to close.

Finish by sewing eyes into place with Black yarn.

ROBIN
the Robin

Robin is more than a little obsessed with his wood-burning stove. All summer he sits on his sofa longing for the temperature to drop low enough so that he can start setting light to his carefully arranged log pile. His wife is starting to get concerned that his self-hewn kindling fixation might have gone too far, especially now he's showing an interest in ripping out the cooker. A quick check on his search history online reveals he has plans for a 'build your own' brick oven in the kitchen. Fortunately for all involved, his wife's favourite foods are best served on a crispy crust, so she might as well just buy him a new axe and start practising her kneading. Who knew robins ate pizza?

YARN REQUIRED

50g TOFT DK yarn Stone
25g TOFT DK yarn Cream
25g TOFT DK yarn Orange

See also *You Will Need* and *Size Options*.

BODY/NECK/HEAD

Work as standard in Cream until after Rnd 15 then continue as follows:

Rnd 16 dc15 Cream, dc15 Orange

Rnds 17-18 dc4 Orange, dc11 Cream, dc15 Orange (2 rnds)

Rnd 19 dc5 Orange, dc10 Cream, dc15 Orange

Rnd 20 dc3, dc2tog Orange, (dc3, dc2tog) twice Cream, (dc3, dc2tog) 3 times Orange (24)

Rnd 21 dc5 Orange, dc7 Stone, dc12 Orange

Next, dc6 in Orange
RESET Rnd

Rnd 22 dc6 Stone, (dc2tog) 9 times Orange (15)

Rnd 23 dc2tog, dc4 Stone, (dc2tog) 4 times, dc1 Orange (10)

Stuff and continue

Rnd 24 dc5 Stone, dc5 Orange

Next, dc5 in Stone
RESET Rnd

Rnd 25 (dc2 into next st) 5 times Orange, (dc2 into next st) 5 times Stone (20)

Rnd 26 (dc3, dc2 into next st) twice, dc2 Orange, dc1, dc2 into next st, (dc3, dc2 into next st) twice Stone (25)

Rnd 27 (dc4, dc2 into next st) twice, dc2 Orange, dc2, dc2 into next st, (dc4, dc2 into next st) twice Stone (30)

Rnd 28 (dc2, dc2 into next st) 4 times, dc2 Orange, dc2 into next st, (dc2, dc2 into next st) 5 times Stone (40)

Rnds 29-31 dc18 Orange, dc22 Stone (3 rnds)

Rnd 32 dc8, dc2tog, dc8 Orange, dc2tog, (dc8, dc2tog) twice Stone (36)

Rnd 33 dc17 Orange, dc19 Stone

Rnd 34 (dc4, dc2tog) twice, dc4 Orange, dc2tog across both colours, (dc4, dc2tog) 3 times Stone (30)

Continue in Stone

Rnd 35 (dc3, dc2tog) 6 times (24)

Rnd 36 (dc2, dc2tog) 6 times (18)

Rnd 37 dc

Rnd 38 (dc2tog) 9 times (9)

Stuff and gather remaining stitches to close.

LEGS (make two)

Work as standard PERCHING in Cream changing to Stone after Rnd 5 working TIBIA as Rnds 1-4 dc (4 rnds) and TARSUS as Rnds 1-5 dc (5 rnds)

WINGS (make two)

Work as standard FLYING in Stone

BEAK

Working in Stone
Ch8 and sl st to join into a circle
Rnd 1 dc
Rnd 2 (dc2, dc2tog) twice (6)
Rnds 3-4 dc (2 rnds)
Rnd 5 (dc1, dc2tog) twice (4)
Rnd 6 (dc2tog) twice (2)
Stuff lightly and sew into position.

TAIL

Working in Cream
Ch16 and sl st to join into a circle
Change to Stone
Rnds 1-6 dc (6 rnds)
Split into two rnds of 8 sts and work each as follows:
Rnds 1-4 dc (4 rnds)
Rnd 5 dc7, dc2 into next st (9)
Rnds 6-8 dc (3 rnds)
Rnd 9 dc8, dc2 into next st (10)
Rnds 10-12 dc (3 rnds)
Rnd 13 (dc3, dc2tog) twice (8)
Rnd 14 (dc2, dc2tog) twice (6)
Rnd 15 (dc2tog) 3 times (3)
Break yarn.
Do not stuff. Sew flat across top to close.

Finish by sewing eyes into place with Black yarn

JORGE
the Jay

Gorgeous Jorge is a singer-songwriter who once produced a catchy one-line tune and now the whole world thinks he's something special. He was in the right place at the right time ten years ago and was delivered the chance for a home-run that would provide him with a nest egg for life. But life is tough when everyone in the business compares what you do now with something critically acclaimed that you did partially by accident a long time ago. To stay relevant against constantly shifting opinion your feathers have to grow bolder, your beak a bit harder, and you have to start to believe that maybe you are somewhat extraordinary after all.

YARN REQUIRED

50g TOFT DK yarn Blue
25g TOFT DK yarn Cream
25g TOFT DK yarn Steel
25g TOFT DK yarn Charcoal

See also *You Will Need* and *Size Options*.

BODY/NECK/HEAD

Work as standard in Cream until after Rnd 21 then continue as follows:

Rnd 22 (dc2tog) 9 times, dc6 (15)

Rnd 23 (dc2tog) 5 times, dc5 (10)

Stuff and continue

Rnd 24 dc

Rnd 25 (dc2 into next st) 4 times, dc1 Charcoal, (dc2 into next st) 5 times Blue (19)

Rnd 26 dc1 Charcoal, (dc2, dc2 into next st) twice, dc2 Cream, dc1 Charcoal, dc2 into next st, (dc3, dc2 into next st) twice Blue (24)

Rnd 27 dc1 Charcoal, dc3, dc2 into next st, dc4, dc2 into next st, dc1 Cream, dc1 Charcoal, (dc2, dc2 into next st) 4 times Blue (30)

Rnd 28 dc1 Charcoal, dc1, dc2 into next st, (dc2, dc2 into next st) 3 times, dc1 Cream, dc1 Charcoal, dc2 into next st, (dc2, dc2 into next st) 5 times Blue (40)

Rnds 29-31 dc1 Charcoal, dc16 Cream, dc1 Charcoal, dc22 Blue (3 rnds)

Rnd 32 dc1 Charcoal, dc6, dc2tog, dc8 Cream, dc1 Charcoal, dc2tog, (dc8, dc2tog) twice Blue (36)

Rnd 33 dc17 Charcoal, dc19 Blue

Continue in Blue

Rnd 34 dc

Rnd 35 (dc2tog, dc4) 3 times, dc2tog, dc16 (32)

Rnd 36 (dc2tog, dc3) 3 times, dc2tog, dc15 (28)

Rnd 37 (dc2tog, dc5) 4 times (24)

Rnd 38 dc

Rnd 39 (dc2tog, dc1) 3 times, dc2tog, dc13 (20)

Rnd 40 (dc2tog) 4 times, dc12 (16)

Rnd 41 dc

Rnd 42 (dc2tog, dc2) 4 times (12)

Rnd 43 (dc2tog, dc1) 4 times (8)

Stuff and gather remaining stitches to close.

LEGS (make two)

Work as standard PERCHING in Cream changing to Steel after Rnd 5 working TIBIA as Rnds 1-7 dc (7 rnds) and TARSUS as Rnds 1-8 dc (8 rnds)

WINGS (make two)

Work as standard FLYING in Blue

BEAK

Working in Steel

Ch12 and sl st to join into a circle

Rnd 1 dc10, dc2tog (11)

Rnd 2 dc9, dc2tog (10)

Rnd 3 dc8, dc2tog (9)

Rnd 4 dc7, dc2tog (8)

Rnd 5 dc6, dc2tog (7)

Rnd 6 dc5, dc2tog (6)

Rnd 7 dc4, dc2tog (5)

Rnd 8 dc3, dc2tog (4)

Stuff lightly and sew into position.

TAIL

Working in Blue

Ch16 and sl st to join into a circle

Rnds 1-3 dc (3 rnds)

Change to Charcoal

Rnd 4 dc

Change to Blue

Rnds 5-6 dc (2 rnds)

Split into two rnds of 8 sts and work each as follows, starting in Blue:

Rnd 1 dc

Change to Charcoal

Rnd 2 dc

Change to Blue

Rnd 3 dc

Rnd 4 dc7, dc2 into next st (9)

Rnd 5 dc

Change to Charcoal

Rnd 6 dc

Change to Blue

Rnd 7 dc

Rnd 8 dc8, dc2 into next st (10)

Rnd 9 dc

Change to Charcoal

Rnd 10 dc

Change to Blue

Rnd 11 dc

Rnd 12 (dc3, dc2tog) twice (8)

Rnd 13 (dc2, dc2tog) twice (6)

Change to Charcoal

Rnd 14 dc

Change to Cream

Rnd 15 dc

Break yarn.

Do not stuff. Sew flat across top to close.

Finish by embroidering face markings with Charcoal and sewing eyes into place with Black yarn.

GARETH
the Puffin

Gareth was caught unawares when he found himself expecting his first puffling when he had barely stopped being one himself. He decided to face the challenge and dived head-first into this unchartered territory. From being a rebellious boy with a brightly coloured beak, he's now a man who can proudly puff out his chest as he takes his son to swimming lessons.

YARN REQUIRED

50g TOFT DK yarn Charcoal
25g TOFT DK yarn Cream
25g TOFT DK yarn Orange
25g TOFT DK yarn Yellow

See also *You Will Need* and *Size Options*.

BODY/NECK/HEAD

Work as standard in Cream until after Rnd 6 then continue as follows:

Rnds 7-8 dc21 Charcoal, dc21 Cream (2 rnds)

Rnd 9 dc1 Cream, dc20 Charcoal, dc21 Cream

Rnd 10 dc1 Cream, dc4, dc2tog, (dc5, dc2tog) twice Charcoal, (dc5, dc2tog) 3 times Cream (36)

Rnds 11-13 dc2 Cream, dc16 Charcoal, dc18 Cream (3 rnds)

Rnd 14 dc3 Cream, dc15 Charcoal, dc18 Cream

Rnd 15 dc3 Cream, dc1, dc2tog, (dc4, dc2tog) twice Charcoal, (dc4, dc2tog) 3 times Cream (30)

Rnd 16 dc3 Cream, dc12 Charcoal, dc15 Cream

Rnds 17-18 dc4 Cream, dc11 Charcoal, dc15 Cream (2 rnds)

Rnd 19 dc5 Cream, dc10 Charcoal, dc15 Cream

Rnd 20 dc3, dc2tog Cream, (dc3, dc2tog) twice Charcoal, (dc3, dc2tog) 3 times Cream (24)

Rnd 21 dc5 Cream, dc7 Charcoal, dc12 Cream

Stuff and continue

Next, dc6 Cream, dc6 Charcoal

RESET Rnd

Rnd 22 (dc2tog) 9 times Cream, dc2, dc2tog, dc2 Charcoal (14)

Rnd 23 (dc1, dc2tog) 3 times Cream, dc1, dc2tog, dc2 Charcoal (10)

Rnd 24 dc6 Cream, dc4 Charcoal

Rnd 25 (dc2 into next st) 7 times Cream, (dc2 into next st) 3 times Charcoal (20)

Rnd 26 (dc3, dc2 into next st) 3 times, dc2 Cream, dc1, dc2 into next st, dc3, dc2 into next st Charcoal (25)

Rnd 27 (dc4, dc2 into next st) 3 times, dc3 Cream, dc2 into next st, dc4, dc2 into next st, dc1 Charcoal (30)

Rnd 28 (dc2, dc2 into next st) 7 times Cream, (dc2, dc2 into next st) 3 times Charcoal (40)

Rnd 29 dc28 Cream, dc12 Charcoal

Rnds 30-31 dc29 Cream, dc11 Charcoal (2 rnds)

Rnd 32 dc1 Charcoal, (dc7, dc2tog) 3 times, dc2 Cream, dc6, dc2tog, dc2 Charcoal (36)

Rnd 33 dc1 Charcoal, dc26 Cream, dc9 Charcoal

Rnd 34 dc2 Charcoal, dc2, dc2tog, (dc4, dc2tog) 3 times, dc3 Cream, dc1, dc2tog, dc4, dc2tog Charcoal (30)

Continue in Charcoal

Rnd 35 (dc3, dc2tog) 6 times (24)

Rnd 36 (dc2, dc2tog) 6 times (18)

Rnd 37 dc

Rnd 38 (dc2tog) 9 times (9)

Stuff and gather remaining stitches to close.

LEGS (make two)

Working in Cream

Ch16 and sl st to join into a circle

Rnds 1-2 dc (2 rnds)

Rnd 3 (dc2, dc2tog) 4 times (12)

Rnd 4 (dc1, dc2tog) 4 times (8)

Then change to Orange and continue to work as standard SWIMMING starting with TIBIA as Rnd 1 dc and TARSUS as Rnds 1-5 dc (5 rnds)

WINGS (make two)

Work as standard FLYING in Charcoal

BEAK

Working in Yellow

Ch24 and sl st to join into a circle

Rnd 1 dc

Change to Charcoal

Rnds 2-3 dc (2 rnds)

Change to Yellow

Rnd 4 (dc6, dc2tog) 3 times (21)

Change to Orange

Rnds 5-7 dc (3 rnds)

Rnd 8 (dc5, dc2tog) 3 times (18)

Rnd 9 (dc4, dc2tog) 3 times (15)

Rnd 10 (dc3, dc2tog) 3 times (12)

Rnd 11 (dc2, dc2tog) 3 times (9)

Rnd 12 (dc1, dc2tog) 3 times (6)

Stuff lightly and sew into position.

TAIL

Working in Charcoal

Ch18 and sl st to join into a circle

Rnds 1-2 dc (2 rnds)

Rnd 3 (dc2, dc2 into next st) 6 times (24)

Rnd 4 dc

Split into three rnds of 8 sts and work each as follows:

Rnds 1-4 dc (4 rnds)

Rnd 5 (dc2tog) 4 times (4)

Break yarn.

Do not stuff. Sew flat across top to close.

Finish by sewing eyes into place with Black yarn.

BEN
the Kingfisher

Ben has a sideways smile that has always sent the girls a-flutter, and is exactly the kind of flirt that has them pecking at each other in his trail. You'll have to try quite hard to find out anything about him that he doesn't want you to know, and so tightly held are certain cards that it leads some to wonder about whether he only whispers all his thoughts to the fish. His staunchly competitive character hides just below the surface of his immaculately presented plumage; so whatever you do don't challenge him to a fishing competition because you might just get more than you bargained for.

YARN REQUIRED

25g TOFT DK yarn Teal
25g TOFT DK yarn Apricot
25g TOFT DK yarn Cream
25g TOFT DK yarn Orange
25g TOFT DK yarn Sapphire

See also *You Will Need* and *Size Options*.

BODY/NECK/HEAD

Work as standard in Apricot until after Rnd 21 then continue as follows:

Rnd 22 (dc2tog) 9 times, dc6 (15)

Rnd 23 (dc2tog) 5 times, dc5 (10)

Stuff and continue

Rnd 24 dc5 Cream, dc5 Teal

Rnd 25 (dc2 into next st) 5 times Cream, (dc2 into next st) 5 times Teal (20)

Rnd 26 (dc3, dc2 into next st) twice, dc2 Cream, dc1, dc2 into next st, (dc3, dc2 into next st) twice Teal (25)

Rnd 27 (dc4, dc2 into next st) 5 times Teal (30)

Rnd 28 (dc2, dc2 into next st) 4 times, dc2 Cream, dc2 into next st, (dc2, dc2 into next st) 5 times Teal (40)

Rnds 29-31 dc18 Apricot, dc22 Teal (3 rnds)

Rnd 32 dc8, dc2tog, dc8 Apricot, dc2tog, (dc8, dc2tog) twice Teal (36)

Rnd 33 dc17 Apricot, dc19 Teal

Continue in Teal

Rnd 34 (dc4, dc2tog) 6 times (30)

Rnd 35 (dc3, dc2tog) 6 times (24)

Rnd 36 (dc2, dc2tog) 6 times (18)

Rnd 37 dc

Rnd 38 (dc2tog) 9 times (9)

Stuff and gather remaining stitches to close.

LEGS (make two)

Work as standard PERCHING in Apricot changing to Orange after Rnd 3 working TIBIA as Rnds 1-2 dc (2 rnds) and TARSUS as Rnds 1-4 dc (4 rnds)

WINGS (make two)

Working in Teal

Begin by dc6 into ring

Rnd 1 dc2, (dc2 into next st) twice, dc2 (8)

Rnd 2 dc3, (dc2 into next st) twice, dc3 (10)

Rnd 3 dc4, (dc2 into next st) twice, dc4 (12)

Rnd 4 dc5, (dc2 into next st) twice, dc5 (14)

Rnd 5 dc6, (dc2 into next st) twice, dc6 (16)

Rnd 6 dc7, (dc2 into next st) twice, dc7 (18)

Rnd 7 dc8, (dc2 into next st) twice, dc8 (20)

Rnds 8-17 dc (10 rnds)

Rnd 18 dc1, (dc2tog) twice, dc10, (dc2tog) twice, dc1 (16)

Rnd 19 dc1, (dc2tog) twice, dc6, (dc2tog) twice, dc1 (12)

Rnd 20 dc

Break yarn, gather stitches. Do not stuff.

Sew down the edges of the two wings to join them together before sewing into position.

BEAK

Working in Sapphire

Ch18 and sl st to join into a circle

Rnds 1-4 dc (4 rnds)

Rnd 5 (dc4, dc2tog) 3 times (15)

Rnds 6-8 dc (3 rnds)

Rnd 9 (dc3, dc2tog) 3 times (12)

Rnds 10-11 dc (2 rnds)

Rnd 12 (dc2, dc2tog) 3 times (9)

Rnds 13-14 dc (2 rnds)

Rnd 15 (dc1, dc2tog) 3 times (6)

Rnd 16 dc

Rnd 17 (dc2tog) 3 times (3)

Stuff lightly and sew into position.

TAIL

Working in Apricot

Ch18 and sl st to join into a circle

Change to Teal

Rnds 1-2 dc (2 rnds)

Rnd 3 (dc2, dc2 into next st) 6 times (24)

Rnd 4 dc

Split into three rnds of 8 sts and work each as follows:

Rnds 1-4 dc (4 rnds)

Rnd 5 (dc2tog) 4 times (4)

Break yarn.

Do not stuff. Sew flat across top to close.

Finish by sewing eyes into place with Black yarn.

YOLANDA
the Cockatiel

Yolanda is an unsung superhero to three boys who lives the busiest of days and boasts the largest odd-sock pile in the country. She counts herself as very lucky that she has the kind of hair that means she can do it with one hand while making packed lunches with the other. It might give the appearance of a perfectly coiffed style, but in reality she knows that's how it looks when she prises her eyes open early every morning and rolls out of bed. Similarly she's blessed with rosy cheeks that mean she barely takes a glance in a mirror in the morning in between checking everyone has brushed their teeth before heading out the door. A natural beauty that's the best mum her boys could wish for.

YARN REQUIRED

50g TOFT DK yarn Shale
25g TOFT DK yarn Primrose
25g TOFT DK yarn Pink
25g TOFT DK yarn Cream
25g TOFT DK yarn Orange

See also *You Will Need* and *Size Options*.

BODY/NECK/HEAD

Work as standard in Shale changing to Primrose after Rnd 23

LEGS (make two)

Working in Shale

Ch12 and sl st to join into a circle

Rnds 1-8 dc (8 rnds)

Change to Pink

Rnd 9 (dc2tog) 6 times (6)

Rnds 10-18 dc (9 rnds)

Next, ch6 and sl st across to other side of rnd to form two 8-st rnds at right angles to the leg when working either side of the chain.

Work each rnd as follows:

Rnd 1 dc8 (2 from rnd, 6 on chain)

Rnd 2 (dc1, dc2 into next st) 4 times (12)

Split into two rnds of 6 sts and work each as follows:

Rnds 1-4 dc (4 rnds)

Rnd 5 (dc2, dc2 into next st) twice (8)

Rnds 6-7 dc (2 rnds)

Rnd 8 (dc2, dc2tog) twice (6)

Break yarn, stuff toes lightly and gather stitches to close.

Lightly stuff thigh and sew flat across top to close.

CLAWS

Working in Shale

Sl st into position on the end of each toe, ch3 and sl st 1, htr1 back down chain

Break yarn and repeat on all toes.

WINGS (make two)

Work as standard FLYING in Cream changing to Shale after Rnd 11

BEAK

Working in Shale

Ch15 and sl st to join into a circle

Rnd 1 dc

Rnd 2 (dc1, dc2tog) 3 times, dc6 (12)

Rnd 3 (dc2tog) 3 times, dc6 (9)

Rnd 4 (dc1, dc2tog) 3 times (6)

Rnd 5 (dc2tog) 3 times (3)

Stuff lightly and sew into position.

CREST

Work a line of six feathers along the top of the head, starting with Primrose at the front of the head and alternating between Primrose and Cream. Sl st into position at one side and work one in Primrose and one in Cream of each length.

Ch15 and sl st 2, dc2, htr2, tr4, dtr4 back down chain, break yarn.

Ch13 and sl st 2, dc2, htr2, tr2, dtr4 back down chain, break yarn.

Ch11 and sl st 2, dc2, htr2, tr2, dtr2 back down chain, break yarn.

CHEEK PATCHES (make two)

Working in Orange

Begin by dc6 into ring

Rnd 1 (dc1, dc2 into next st) 3 times (9)

Sew into position on either side of head.

TAIL

Working in Shale

Ch16 and sl st to join into a circle

Rnds 1-6 dc (6 rnds)

Split into two rnds of 8 sts and work each as follows:

Rnds 1-7 dc (7 rnds)

Rnd 8 dc7, dc2 into next st (9)

Rnds 9-14 dc (6 rnds)

Rnd 15 dc8, dc2 into next st (10)

Rnds 16-18 dc (3 rnds)

Rnd 19 (dc3, dc2tog) twice (8)

Rnd 20 (dc2, dc2tog) twice (6)

Rnd 21 (dc2tog) 3 times (3)

Break yarn.

Do not stuff. Sew flat across top to close.

Finish by sewing eyes into place with Black yarn.

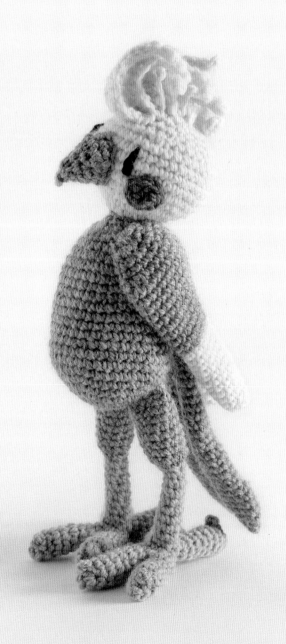

GIANNI
the Lovebird

Gianni loves birds. He loves being around birds, talking to birds and especially dancing with other birds; well the three things are inextricably linked, really. When he sees another bird he just has to talk to them, and once he talks to them he gets a little carried away. You see, when Gianni chats he gestures with his entire body from his eyes to his claws, and the more engaging the conversation the more his shoulders move, and wings flap, until eventually he's dancing without even realising (and all that was just over ordering some pasta from the waitress).

YARN REQUIRED

50g TOFT DK yarn Lime
25g TOFT DK yarn Sage
25g TOFT DK yarn Peach
25g TOFT DK yarn Silver
25g TOFT DK yarn Oatmeal

See also *You Will Need* and *Size Options*.

BODY/NECK/HEAD

Work as standard in Sage until after Rnd 16 then continue as follows:

Change to Peach

Rnds 17-19 dc (3 rnds)

Rnd 20 (dc3, dc2tog) 6 times (24)

Rnd 21 dc

Change to Lime

Rnd 22 dc6 Lime, (dc2tog) 9 times Peach (15)

Rnd 23 dc2tog, dc4 Lime, (dc2tog) 4 times, dc1 Peach (10)

Stuff and continue

Rnd 24 dc5 Lime, dc5 Peach

Next, dc5 in Lime

RESET Rnd

Rnd 25 (dc2 into next st) 5 times Peach, (dc2 into next st) 5 times Lime (20)

Rnd 26 (dc3, dc2 into next st) twice, dc2 Peach, dc1, dc2 into next st (dc3, dc2 into next st) twice Lime (25)

Rnd 27 (dc4, dc2 into next st) twice, dc2 Peach, dc2, dc2 into next st (dc4, dc2 into next st) twice Lime (30)

Rnd 28 (dc2, dc2 into next st) 4 times, dc2 Peach, dc2 into next st, (dc2, dc2 into next st) 5 times Lime (40)

Rnds 29-31 dc18 Peach, dc22 Lime (3 rnds)

Rnd 32 dc8, dc2tog, dc8 Peach, dc2tog, (dc8, dc2tog) twice Lime (36)

Rnd 33 dc17 Peach, dc19 Lime

Rnd 34 (dc4, dc2tog) twice, dc4 Peach, dc2tog across both colours, (dc4, dc2tog) 3 times Lime (30)

Continue in Lime

Rnd 35 (dc3, dc2tog) 6 times (24)

Rnd 36 (dc2, dc2tog) 6 times (18)

Rnd 37 dc

Rnd 38 (dc2tog) 9 times (9)

Stuff and gather remaining stitches to close.

LEGS (make two)

Working in Lime

Ch12 and sl st to join into a circle

Rnds 1-4 dc (4 rnds)

Rnd 5 (dc2tog) 6 times (6)

Change to Silver

Rnds 6-14 dc (9 rnds)

Next, ch6 and sl st across to other side of rnd to form two 8-st rnds at right angles to the leg when working either side of the chain.

Work each rnd as follows:

Rnd 1 dc8 (2 from rnd, 6 on chain)

Rnd 2 (dc1, dc2 into next st) 4 times (12)

Split into two rnds of 6 sts and work each as follows:

Rnds 1-4 dc (4 rnds)

Rnd 5 (dc2, dc2 into next st) twice (8)

Rnds 6-7 dc (2 rnds)

Rnd 8 (dc2, dc2tog) twice (6)

Rnd 9 (dc1, dc2tog) twice (4)

Break yarn.

Lightly stuff thigh and sew flat across top to close.

CLAWS

Working in Oatmeal

Sl st into position on the end of each toe, ch3 and sl st 1, htr1 back down chain

Break yarn and repeat on all toes.

WINGS (make two)

Work as standard FLYING in Lime

BEAK

Working in Oatmeal

Ch15 and sl st to join into a circle

Rnds 1-2 dc (2 rnds)

Rnd 3 dc3, (dc2tog) 6 times (9)

Rnd 4 dc

Rnd 5 dc3, (dc2tog) 3 times (6)

Rnd 6 dc

Rnd 7 (dc2tog) 3 times (3)

Stuff lightly and sew into position.

TAIL

Working in Sage

Ch18 and sl st to join into a circle

Change to Lime

Rnds 1-3 dc (3 rnds)

Rnd 4 (dc2, dc2 into next st) 6 times (24)

Rnd 5 dc

Split into three rnds of 8 sts and work each as follows:

Rnd 1-7 dc (7 rnds)

Rnd 8 (dc2, dc2tog) twice (6)

Rnd 9 (dc2tog) 3 times (3)

Break yarn.

Do not stuff. Sew flat across top to close.

Stuff and sew up your bird and then continue to add details.

Sew eyes into place with Black yarn.

FEATHERS

Work ch4 CHAIN LOOPS in Peach over the face and chest, and ch5 CHAIN LOOPS in Lime over the back of the head and neck.

PUTU
the Lesser Bird of Paradise

Putu is an unlikely athlete, propelled down the track almost involuntarily by those long legs that seems to have outgrown everything but his tail. The first born to a very large clutch of beautiful birds, he honed his reaction times and speed by chasing after a dozen other long tail feathers while his parents were out working to keep food on the table. His favourite time of the week comes when he gets to forget everyone else for just a few minutes of focus on the finish line. After carefully pinning a number to the front of his chest, he stops for a deep breath on his marks before running past in a flash of feathers so quick you won't have a chance to spot the beautiful smile matching them.

YARN REQUIRED

50g TOFT DK yarn Beetroot
25g TOFT DK yarn Green
25g TOFT DK yarn Yellow
25g TOFT DK yarn Silver
25g TOFT DK yarn Cream

See also *You Will Need* and *Size Options*.

BODY/NECK/HEAD

Work as standard in Beetroot until after Rnd 21 then continue as follows:

Rnd 22 (dc2tog) 9 times, dc6 (15)

Rnd 23 (dc2tog) 5 times, dc5 (10)

Stuff and continue

Rnd 24 dc

Rnd 25 (dc2 into next st) 5 times Green, (dc2 into next st) 5 times Yellow (20)

Rnd 26 (dc3, dc2 into next st) twice, dc2 Green, dc1, dc2 into next st, (dc3, dc2 into next st) twice Yellow (25)

Rnd 27 (dc4, dc2 into next st) twice, dc2 Green, dc2, dc2 into next st, (dc4, dc2 into next st) twice Yellow (30)

Rnd 28 (dc2, dc2 into next st) 4 times, dc2 Green, dc2 into next st, (dc2, dc2 into next st) 5 times Yellow (40)

Rnds 29-31 dc18 Green, dc22 Yellow (3 rnds)

Rnd 32 dc8, dc2tog, dc8 Green, dc2tog, (dc8, dc2tog) twice Yellow (36)

Rnd 33 dc17 Green, dc19 Yellow

Rnd 34 (dc4, dc2tog) twice, dc4 Green, dc2tog across both colours, (dc4, dc2tog) 3 times Yellow (30)

Continue in Yellow

Rnd 35 (dc3, dc2tog) 6 times (24)

Rnd 36 (dc2, dc2tog) 6 times (18)

Rnd 37 dc

Rnd 38 (dc2tog) 9 times (9)

Stuff and gather remaining stitches to close.

LEGS (make two)

Work as standard PERCHING in Beetroot changing to Silver after Rnd 5 working TIBIA as Rnds 1-7 dc (7 rnds) and TARSUS as Rnds 1-8 dc (8 rnds)

WINGS (make two)

Work as standard FLYING in Beetroot

BEAK

Working in Silver

Ch12 and sl st to join into a circle

Rnd 1 dc

Rnd 2 (dc4, dc2tog) twice (10)

Rnd 3 (dc3, dc2tog) twice (8)

Rnd 4 (dc2, dc2tog) twice (6)

Rnd 5 (dc2tog) twice, (dc2 into next st) twice (6)

Rnd 6 (dc2tog) twice, dc2 (4)

Stuff lightly and sew into position.

TOP PLUMAGE

Working in Yellow

Ch12 and sl st to join into a circle

Rnds 1-6 dc (6 rnds)

Split into two rnds of 6 sts and work each as follows:

*Rnds 1-15 dc (15 rnds)

Rnd 16 dc5, dc2 into next st (7)

Rnds 17-21 dc (5 rnds)

Rnd 22 dc6, dc2 into next st (8)

Rnds 23-27 dc (5 rnds)

Rnd 28 dc7, dc2 into next st (9)

Rnds 29-33 dc (5 rnds)

Rnd 34 dc8, dc2 into next st (10)

Rnds 35-39 dc (5 rnds)

Rnd 40 (dc3, dc2tog) twice (8)

Rnd 41 (dc2, dc2tog) twice (6)

Rnd 42 (dc1, dc2tog) twice (4)

Break yarn.

Work feathers around the bottom 12 rnds by ch6 and sl st 5 down chain, sl st 2 along tail

BOTTOM PLUMAGE

Working in Cream

Ch18 and sl st to join into a circle

Rnds 1-6 dc (6 rnds)

Split into three rnds of 6 sts and work each as TOP PLUMAGE from *

Work feathers along the two outside edges by ch6 and sl st 5 down chain, sl st 2 along tail

TAIL

Working in Beetroot

Ch16 and sl st to join into a circle

Rnds 1-6 dc (6 rnds)

Split into two rnds of 8 sts and work each as follows:

Rnds 1-4 dc (4 rnds)

Rnd 5 dc7, dc2 into next st (9)

Rnds 6-8 dc (3 rnds)

Rnd 9 dc8, dc2 into next st (10)

Rnds 10-12 dc (3 rnds)

Rnd 13 (dc3, dc2tog) twice (8)

Rnd 14 (dc2, dc2tog) twice (6)

Rnd 15 (dc2tog) 3 times (3)

Break yarn.

Do not stuff. Sew flat across top to close.

Sew the tail into position followed by bottom and top plumage with the Yellow above the Cream.

Finish by sewing eyes into place with Black yarn.

JACK
the Macaw

Jack has recently become a swashbuckling entertainer, following a dramatic fall from grace (off the stage and into the orchestra pit) on the opening night of his big break. A plausible Iago he ain't. It turns out he is far more lovable rogue than maligned plunderer, and the sound of fledglings' giddy peeping fills his big heart with tenderness, and that overwhelming emotion now safely locked up in his chest has superseded any desire to break a leg. Once his peg is strapped on and he's hobbling in front of the bouncy castle he'll walk the plank any number of times for giggling tweets.

YARN REQUIRED

50g TOFT DK yarn Yellow
25g TOFT DK yarn Turquoise
25g TOFT DK yarn Steel
25g TOFT DK yarn Charcoal
25g TOFT DK yarn Cream
25g TOFT DK yarn Lime

See also *You Will Need* and *Size Options*.

BODY/NECK/HEAD

Work as standard in Yellow until after Rnd 21 then continue as follows:

Rnd 22 (dc2tog) 9 times, dc6 (15)

Rnd 23 (dc2tog) 5 times, dc5 (10)

Stuff and continue

Rnd 24 dc5 Yellow, dc5 Turquoise

Rnd 25 (dc2 into next st) 5 times Yellow, (dc2 into next st) 5 times Turquoise (20)

Rnd 26 (dc3, dc2 into next st) twice dc2 Yellow, dc1, dc2 into next st, (dc3, dc2 into next st) twice Turquoise (25)

Rnd 27 (dc4, dc2 into next st) twice, dc2 Yellow, dc2, dc2 into next st, (dc4, dc2 into next st) twice Turquoise (30)

Rnd 28 (dc2, dc2 into next st) 4 times, dc2 Yellow, dc2 into next st, (dc2, dc2 into next st) 5 times Turquoise (40)

Rnd 29 dc18 Charcoal, dc22 Turquoise

Rnds 30-31 dc18 Cream, dc22 Turquoise (2 rnds)

Rnd 32 dc8, dc2tog, dc8 Cream, dc2tog, (dc8, dc2tog) twice Turquoise (36)

Rnd 33 dc17 Cream, dc19 Lime

Rnd 34 (dc4, dc2tog) twice dc4 Cream, dc2tog across both colours, (dc4, dc2tog) 3 times Lime (30)

Continue in Lime

Rnd 35 (dc3, dc2tog) 6 times (24)

Rnd 36 (dc2, dc2tog) 6 times (18)

Rnd 37 dc

Rnd 38 (dc2tog) 9 times (9)

Stuff and gather remaining stitches to close.

LEGS (make two)

Work as standard CLIMBING in Yellow changing to Steel after Rnd 9

WINGS (make two)

Work as standard SOARING in Turquoise

BEAK

Working in Charcoal

Ch24 and sl st to join into a circle

Rnds 1-3 dc rnds (3 rnds)

Rnd 4 (dc1, dc2tog) 8 times (16)

Rnd 5 (dc1, dc2tog) 5 times, dc1 (11)

Rnd 6 dc

Rnd 7 dc2tog, dc4, dc2 into next st, dc2, dc2tog (10)

Fold end in half to close and oversew flat down the beak, then sew a few extra stitches into the last stitch to create hook end.

Stuff lightly and sew into position.

LOWER TAIL

Working in Yellow

Ch16 and sl st to join into a circle

Rnds 1-2 dc (2 rnds)

Rnd 3 (dc1, dc2 into next st) 8 times (24)

Rnds 4-5 dc (2 rnds)

Split into three rnds of 8 sts and work each as follows:

Rnds 1-3 dc (3 rnds)

Rnd 4 dc7, dc2 into next st (9)

Rnds 5-7 dc (3 rnds)

Rnd 8 dc8, dc2 into next st (10)

Rnds 9-11 dc (3 rnds)

Rnd 12 (dc3, dc2tog) twice (8)

Rnd 13 (dc2, dc2tog) twice (6)

Rnd 14 (dc2tog) 3 times (3)

Break yarn.

Do not stuff. Sew flat across top to close.

UPPER TAIL

Working in Turquoise

Ch16 and sl st to join into a circle

Rnds 1-6 dc (6 rnds)

Split into two rnds of 8 sts and work each as follows:

Rnds 1-4 dc (4 rnds)

Rnd 5 dc7, dc2 into next st (9)

Rnds 6-8 dc (3 rnds)

Rnd 9 dc8, dc2 into next st (10)

Rnds 10-12 dc (3 rnds)

Rnd 13 (dc3, dc2tog) twice (8)

Rnd 14 (dc2, dc2tog) twice (6)

Rnd 15 (dc2tog) 3 times (3)

Break yarn.

Do not stuff. Sew flat across top to close.

Sew both tail pieces into position with the Turquoise above the Yellow.

Finish by sewing eyes into place with Black yarn.

RENÉE

the Shalow's Turaco

This year Renée's made a resolution to put her scrawniest foot forward and start everything all over again. Too long has she flapped around worrying about making the right impression as many less fine-feathered have soared past her flying high. With a new-found confidence that some will love her (even if others may not), her broken wing's forgotten with one glance at her crafted crest. Preened, pleased and proud, she's ready to strut out of the shadows and into the spotlight.

YARN REQUIRED

50g TOFT DK yarn Chive
25g TOFT DK yarn Green
25g TOFT DK yarn Steel
25g TOFT DK yarn Cream
25g TOFT DK yarn Orange

See also *You Will Need* and *Size Options*.

BODY/NECK/HEAD

Work as standard in Green changing to Chive after Rnd 6 until Rnd 21 then continue as follows:

Rnd 22 (dc2tog) 9 times, dc6 (15)

Rnd 23 (dc2tog) 5 times, dc5 (10)

Rnd 24 dc

Rnd 25 (dc2 into next st) 10 times (20)

Rnd 26 (dc3, dc2 into next st) 5 times (25)

Rnd 27 (dc4, dc2 into next st) 5 times (30)

Rnd 28 (dc2, dc2 into next st) 10 times (40)

Rnd 29 dc6 Cream, dc6 Chive, dc6 Cream, dc22 Chive

Rnds 30-31 dc1 Chive, dc3 Orange, dc2 Cream, dc6 Chive, dc2 Cream, dc3 Orange, dc23 Chive (2 rnds)

Continue in Chive

Rnd 32 (dc8, dc2tog) 4 times (36)

Rnd 33 dc

Rnd 34 (dc4, dc2tog) 6 times (30)

Rnd 35 (dc3, dc2tog) 6 times (24)

Rnd 36 (dc2, dc2tog) 6 times (18)

Rnd 37 dc

Rnd 38 (dc2tog) 9 times (9)

Stuff and gather remaining stitches to close.

LEGS (make two)

Work as standard PERCHING in Green changing to Steel after Rnd 5 working TIBIA as Rnds 1-7 dc (7 rnds) and TARSUS as Rnds 1-8 dc (8 rnds)

WINGS (make two)

Work as standard FLYING in Green changing to Chive after Rnd 19

BEAK

Working in Orange

Ch15 and sl st to join into a circle

Rnd 1 dc

Rnd 2 (dc3, dc2tog) 3 times (12)

Rnd 3 (dc2, dc2tog) 3 times (9)

Rnd 4 dc

Rnd 5 (dc1, dc2tog) 3 times (6)

Stuff lightly and sew into position.

TAIL

Working in Chive

Ch16 and sl st to join into a circle

Rnds 1-5 dc (5 rnds)

Change to Green

Rnd 6 dc

Split into two rnds of 8 sts and work each as follows:

Rnds 1-4 dc (4 rnds)

Rnd 5 dc7, dc2 into next st (9)

Rnds 6-8 dc (3 rnds)

Rnd 9 dc8, dc2 into next st (10)

Rnds 10-12 dc (3 rnds)

Rnd 13 (dc3, dc2tog) twice (8)

Rnd 14 (dc2, dc2tog) twice (6)

Rnd 15 (dc2tog) 3 times (3)

Break yarn.

Do not stuff. Sew flat across top to close.

CREST

Working in Chive

Sl st into position in the centre of the head approx. 4 rnds up from top of eye patches

Work a row of nine feathers from front to back along top of head as follows:

Work three ch15 SLIP STITCH CHAINS, three ch12 SLIP STITCH CHAINS and three ch9 SLIP STITCH CHAINS

Working in Cream

Work one 3cm (1¼in) KNOT LENGTH to end of each chain

Trim to approx. 1cm (⅓in)

Finish by sewing eyes into place with Black yarn.

KNOT LENGTH

1. Cut a length of yarn and fold in half. Insert hook into stitch or fabric and yarn over with the centre of the length.

2. Bring the loop through the stitch.

3. Pull the cut ends through the loop before pulling tight to secure.

TERENCE
the Budgerigar

Terence is an expert microwave cook who prides himself on managing to produce a roast dinner from just the bottom drawer of his fridge and whatever he's managed to pick up with yellow stickers on at the end of his shift. He's a very friendly bird who twitters on to anyone and everyone all day long as he scans barcode after barcode across his checkout. Regarding himself as an exceptionally astute and frugal grocery shopper, he's always ready to offer advice on savings, voucher codes and ways to make the contents of your basket go much further than you initially thought.

YARN REQUIRED

25g TOFT DK yarn Lime
25g TOFT DK yarn Yellow
25g TOFT DK yarn Shale
25g TOFT DK yarn Teal
25g TOFT DK yarn Charcoal
25g TOFT DK yarn Amethyst

See also *You Will Need* and *Size Options*.

BODY/NECK/HEAD

Work as standard in Lime changing to Yellow after Rnd 20 then continue as follows:

Rnd 21 dc

Rnd 22 (dc2tog) 9 times, dc6 (15)

Rnd 23 (dc2tog) 5 times, dc5 (10)

Stuff and continue

Rnd 24 dc

Rnd 25 (dc2 into next st) 10 times (20)

Rnd 26 (dc3, dc2 into next st) twice, dc2 Yellow, dc1, dc2 into next st, (dc3, dc2 into next st) twice Charcoal (25)

Rnd 27 (dc4, dc2 into next st) 5 times Yellow (30)

Rnd 28 (dc2, dc2 into next st) 4 times, dc2 Yellow, dc2 into next st, (dc2, dc2 into next st) 5 times Charcoal (40)

Rnd 29 dc Yellow

Rnd 30 dc19 Yellow, dc21 Charcoal

Rnd 31 dc Yellow

Rnd 32 dc8, dc2tog, dc8 Yellow, dc2tog, (dc8, dc2tog) twice Charcoal (36)

Rnd 33 dc Yellow

Rnd 34 (dc4, dc2tog) 3 times Yellow, (dc4, dc2tog) 3 times Charcoal (30)

Rnd 35 (dc3, dc2tog) 6 times Yellow (24)

Rnd 36 (dc2, dc2tog) 3 times Yellow, (dc2, dc2tog) 3 times Charcoal (18)

Rnd 37 dc Yellow

Rnd 38 (dc2tog) 5 times Yellow, (dc2tog) 4 times Charcoal (9)

Stuff and gather remaining stitches to close.

LEGS (make two)

Working in Lime

Ch12 and sl st to join into a circle

Rnds 1-3 dc (3 rnds)

Rnd 4 (dc2, dc2tog) 3 times (9)

Rnd 5 (dc1, dc2tog) 3 times (6)

Change to Shale

Rnds 6-8 dc (3 rnds)

Rnd 9 (dc2 into next st) 6 times (12)

Rnds 10-11 dc (2 rnds)

Rnd 12 (dc2tog) 6 times (6)

Rnds 13-16 dc (4 rnds)

Next, ch6 and sl st across to other side of rnd to form two 8-st rnds at right angles to the leg when working either side of the chain.

Work each rnd as follows:

Rnd 1 dc8 (2 from rnd, 6 on chain)

Rnd 2 (dc1, dc2 into next st) 4 times (12)

Split into two rnds of 6 sts and work each as follows:

Rnds 1-4 dc (4 rnds)

Rnd 5 (dc2, dc2 into next st) twice (8)

Rnds 6-7 dc (2 rnds)

Rnd 8 (dc2, dc2tog) twice (6)

Lightly stuff toe and continue

Rnd 9 (dc1, dc2tog) twice (4)

Break yarn.

Lightly stuff thigh and sew flat across top to close.

WINGS (make two)

Work as standard FLYING starting in Charcoal working stripes of 1 rnd Charcoal and 1 rnd Yellow (dc6 into ring counts as first rnd)

BEAK

Working in Teal

Ch5 and work in rows as follows:

Rows 1-2 dc4, turn (2 rows)

Change to Shale

Row 3 dc1, dc2tog, dc1, turn (3)

Rows 4-5 dc3, turn (2 rows)

Break yarn and gather 3 sts at end of beak. Sew top flat into position.

CHEEK PATCHES

Embroider two Amethyst stitches into position on either side of face.

TAIL

Working in Lime

Ch16 and sl st to join into a circle

Rnds 1-4 dc (4 rnds)

Change to Teal

Rnds 5-6 (2 rnds)

Split into two rnds of 8 sts and work each as follows:

Rnds 1-4 dc (4 rnds)

Rnd 5 dc7, dc2 into next st (9)

Rnds 6-8 dc (3 rnds)

Rnd 9 dc8, dc2 into next st (10)

Rnds 10-12 dc (3 rnds)

Rnd 13 (dc3, dc2tog) twice (8)

Rnd 14 (dc2, dc2tog) twice (6)

Rnd 15 (dc2tog) 3 times (3)

Break yarn.

Do not stuff. Sew flat across top to close.

Finish by sewing eyes into place with Black yarn.

ENID
the Long-Eared Owl

At school, Enid's teachers always speculated that she was wise beyond her years and her breathy hoots might one day make history. So hard has she fought for what she believes in that she has had to sacrifice a lot of things on her flight path into Parliament. Her entire career she has kept her wide eyes firmly fixed on the glass ceiling above her, which she fully intends to fly straight through when she gets there. The moment she stood up in the debating society and proposed the motion 'the more mice I meet, the more I eat nuts', her family should have foreseen that she was a pretty extraordinary owl.

YARN REQUIRED

50g TOFT DK yarn Stone
25g TOFT DK yarn Chestnut
25g TOFT DK yarn Oatmeal

See also *You Will Need* and *Size Options*.

SPOT PATTERN

Work 4 sts Stone, 2 sts Chestnut

BODY/NECK/HEAD

Work as standard starting in Stone working 1 rnd SPOT PATTERN and 1 rnd Stone

LEGS (make two)

Work as standard GRASPING in Stone changing to Oatmeal after Rnd 14 and to Chestnut after Rnd 9 of toes

BACK TOE

Working in Oatmeal
SLIP STITCH TRAVERSE a 6-st ring on back of foot and work as follows:
Rnds 1-2 dc (2 rnds)
Rnd 3 (dc1, dc2tog) twice (4)
Change to Chestnut
Rnd 4 dc
Rnd 5 (dc2tog) twice (2)
Break yarn.

Lightly stuff thigh and sew flat across top to close.

WINGS (make two)

Work as standard SOARING with SPOT PATTERN

EYE PATCHES (make two)

Working in Oatmeal
Begin by dc6 into ring
Rnd 1 (dc2 into next st) 6 times (12)
Rnd 2 (dc1, dc2 into next st) 6 times (18)
Change to Chestnut
Rnd 3 dc9 (incomplete rnd)
Break yarn.

Sew the two patches together with the two Chestnut stitches joined in the middle.

EARS

Working In Chestnut
Sl st into the first Chestnut stitch on the eye patches, ch9 and dc2, htr2, tr2, dtr2 back down chain
Miss 3 sts along eye patches and sl st into next st, dc6 along the top of the eye patches
Ch9 and dc2, htr2, tr2, dtr2 back down chain, sl st into last Chestnut stitch, break yarn.

Sew into position on head, then work a line of sl st along the edge of the ears in Stone.

BEAK

Working in Chestnut
Sl st into position between the eye patches, ch5 and sl st 1, dc2 back down chain, sl st into head
Use the ends to sew the beak flat.

TAIL

Working in Stone
Ch16 and sl st to join into a circle
Continue working in SPOT PATTERN
Rnds 1-2 dc (2 rnds)
Rnd 3 (dc1, dc2 into next st) 8 times (24)
Rnds 4-5 dc (2 rnds)
Split into three rnds of 8 sts and work right and left rnds as follows:
Rnds 1-4 dc (4 rnds)
Rnd 5 dc7, dc2 into next st (9)
Rnd 6 dc
Rnd 7 dc8, dc2 into next st (10)
Rnds 8-10 dc (3 rnds)
Rnd 11 (dc3, dc2tog) twice (8)
Rnd 12 (dc2, dc2tog) twice (6)
Rnd 13 (dc2tog) 3 times (3)
Break yarn.

Rejoin and work central 8-st rnd as follows:
Rnds 1-4 dc (4 rnds)
Rnd 5 dc7, dc2 into next st (9)
Rnds 6-9 dc (4 rnds)
Rnd 10 dc8, dc2 into next st (10)
Rnds 11-13 dc (3 rnds)
Rnd 14 (dc3, dc2tog) twice (8)
Rnd 15 (dc2, dc2tog) twice (6)
Rnd 16 (dc2tog) 3 times (3)
Break yarn.
Do not stuff. Sew flat across top to close.

Finish by sewing eyes into place with Black yarn.

EZRA
the Gouldian Finch

Ezra is an antique hunter with an eye for a bargain and a penchant for very old typewriters upon which to punch out his latest conceptual poem. A very liberal character who funds his British Summertime touring of literary festivals by scratting around in junk shops all winter, and being the earliest bird in the queue at every car-boot sale in the county. Every horizontal surface in his life is covered with eclectic treasure, from his under-used dining table to the dashboard of his beaten-up camper van, living in spaces full of excess and flamboyance. Inspired by unusual *objets d'art* from centuries gone by, his resulting verse is free from the constraints of punctuation and as colourful as it comes.

YARN REQUIRED

25g TOFT DK yarn Yellow
25g TOFT DK yarn Amethyst
25g TOFT DK yarn Turquoise
25g TOFT DK yarn Ruby
25g TOFT DK yarn Lime
25g TOFT DK yarn Oatmeal
25g TOFT DK yarn Charcoal

See also *You Will Need* and *Size Options*.

BODY/NECK/HEAD

Work as standard in Yellow changing to Amethyst after Rnd 11 until Rnd 21 then continue as follows:

Rnd 22 (dc2tog) 9 times, dc6 (15)

Rnd 23 (dc2tog) 5 times, dc5 (10)

Stuff and continue

Rnd 24 dc

Change to Turquoise

Rnd 25 (dc2 into next st) 10 times (20)

Rnd 26 (dc3, dc2 into next st) 5 times (25)

Rnd 27 (dc4, dc2 into next st) 5 times (30)

Rnd 28 (dc2, dc2 into next st) 10 times (40)

Rnd 29 dc18 Charcoal, dc22 Turquoise

Rnds 30-31 dc18 Ruby, dc5 Turquoise, dc12 Lime, dc5 Turquoise (2 rnds)

Rnd 32 dc8, dc2tog, dc8 Ruby, dc2tog, dc3 Turquoise, dc5, dc2tog, dc5 Lime, dc2tog, dc3 Turquoise (36)

Rnd 33 dc17 Ruby, dc4 Turquoise, dc11 Lime, dc4 Turquoise

Rnd 34 (dc4, dc2tog) twice, dc5 Ruby, dc2tog, dc2 Turquoise, dc2, dc2tog, dc4, dc2tog, dc1 Lime, dc2, dc2tog Turquoise (30)

Rnd 35 (dc3, dc2tog) 3 times, dc3 Turquoise, dc2tog, dc3, dc2tog, dc2 Lime, dc1, dc2tog Turquoise (24)

Rnd 36 (dc2, dc2tog) 3 times, dc3 Turquoise, dc2tog, dc2, dc2tog, dc1 Lime, dc2tog Turquoise (18)

Continue in Turquoise

Rnd 37 dc

Rnd 38 (dc2tog) 9 times (9)

Stuff and gather remaining stitches to close.

LEGS (make two)

Work as standard PERCHING in Yellow changing to Oatmeal after Rnd 5 working TIBIA as Rnds 1-4 dc (4 rnds) and TARSUS as Rnds 1-4 dc (4 rnds)

WINGS (make two)

Work as standard FLYING in Lime

BEAK

Working in Oatmeal

Ch15 and sl st to join into a circle

Rnd 1 dc

Rnd 2 (dc3, dc2tog) 3 times (12)

Rnd 3 (dc2, dc2tog) 3 times (9)

Rnd 4 dc

Rnd 5 (dc1, dc2tog) 3 times (6)

Stuff lightly and sew into position.

TAIL

Working in Yellow

Ch18 and sl st to join into a circle

Change to Turquoise

Rnds 1-3 dc (3 rnds)

Rnd 4 (dc2, dc2 into next st) 6 times (24)

Rnd 5 dc

Split into three rnds of 8 sts and work first rnd as follows:

Rnds 1-7 dc (7 rnds)

Rnd 8 (dc2, dc2tog) twice (6)

Rnd 9 (dc2tog) 3 times (3)

Break yarn.

Work next 8-st rnd as follows:

Rnds 1-4 dc (4 rnds)

Rnd 5 dc7, dc2 into next st (9)

Rnds 6-8 dc (3 rnds)

Rnd 9 dc8, dc2 into next st (10)

Rnds 10-12 dc (3 rnds)

Rnd 13 (dc3, dc2tog) twice (8)

Rnd 14 (dc2, dc2tog) twice (6)

Rnd 15 (dc2tog) 3 times (3)

Break yarn.

Work last 8-st rnd as follows:

Rnds 1-7 dc (7 rnds)

Rnd 8 (dc2, dc2tog) twice (6)

Rnd 9 (dc2tog) 3 times (3)

Break yarn.

Do not stuff. Sew flat across top to close.

Finish by sewing eyes into place with Black yarn.

ROHIT
the Peacock

Rohit has only just broken the habit of looking over his shoulder to see how long his tail has grown that day. His personal challenge is to cultivate a character big enough to match his plumage. Despite being scared of flying he's taking his first trip abroad this year to meet new people, eat new things and try out the power of his enormous train. His only concern is getting far enough away so that the all-seeing eyes of his mother aren't still peering over his shoulder.

YARN REQUIRED

50g TOFT DK yarn Blue
50g TOFT DK yarn Green
25g TOFT DK yarn Stone
25g TOFT DK yarn Cream
25g TOFT DK yarn Charcoal

See also *You Will Need* and *Size Options*.

BODY/NECK/HEAD

Work as standard in Blue working NECK as Rnds 1-4 dc (4 rnds)

LEGS (make two)

Work as standard PERCHING in Blue changing to Stone after Rnd 5 working TIBIA as Rnds 1-9 dc (9 rnds) and TARSUS as Rnds 1-10 dc (10 rnds)

WINGS (make two)

Work as standard FLYING with a colour pattern of 3 sts Cream, 2 sts Charcoal throughout

BEAK

Working in Stone
Ch15 and sl st to join into a circle
Rnd 1 dc
Rnd 2 (dc3, dc2tog) 3 times (12)
Rnd 3 dc
Rnd 4 (dc2, dc2tog) 3 times (9)
Rnds 5-6 dc (2 rnds)
Rnd 7 (dc1, dc2tog) 3 times (6)
Rnds 8-10 dc (3 rnds)
Stuff lightly and sew into position.

HEAD FEATHERS

Working in Stone
Work five ch9 SLIP STITCH CHAINS into top of head.
Then work a bobble onto the end of each feather as follows:
Working in Blue
Sl st into position on the end of feather, MB, sl st into feather, break yarn.

TAIL (make three)

Working in Green
Ch18 and sl st to join into a circle
Rnd 1 dc
Rnd 2 (dc2, dc2 into next st) 6 times (24)
Rnds 3-5 dc (3 rnds)
Split into three rnds of 8 sts and work each as follows:
Rnds 1-8 dc (8 rnds)
Rnd 9 dc7, dc2 into next st (9)
Rnds 10-11 dc (2 rnds)
Rnd 12 dc8, dc2 into next st (10)
Rnd 13 dc
Rnd 14 (dc4, dc2 into next st) twice (12)
Rnds 15-16 dc (2 rnds)
Rnd 17 (dc3, dc2 into next st) 3 times (15)
Rnds 18-19 dc (2 rnds)
Rnd 20 (dc1, dc2tog) 5 times (10)
Rnd 21 (dc2tog) 5 times (5)
Break yarn.
Do not stuff. Sew flat across top to close.

OCELLI/EYESPOTS (make nine)

Working in Blue
Begin by dc6 into ring
Change to Stone
Rnd 1 (dc2 into next st) 6 times (12)
Sew into position on ends of tail.

Finish by sewing eyes into place with Black yarn.

Working in Cream
Embroider stitches into a triangle shape around the eyes.

LEVI
the Red and Yellow Barbet

This precision ironer folds t-shirts in a way that he can fit twice more in his drawer than either you or I. He simply detests having a feather out of place, and so everything from his pillows to his pants undergo steaming, pressing with him finishing off the corners by hand for good measure. That said, his laundry skills may be faultless but they are certainly not swift, so if you're ever given an invitation for a weekend at his, then make sure you give plenty of notice so your sheets can receive the full treatment. There's nothing spontaneous about this perfectly preened bird, but the resulting perfection is worth the painstaking attention to detail getting there.

YARN REQUIRED

25g TOFT DK yarn Yellow
25g TOFT DK yarn Ruby
25g TOFT DK yarn Coral
25g TOFT DK yarn Charcoal
25g TOFT DK yarn Cream

See also *You Will Need* and *Size Options*.

BODY/NECK/HEAD

Work as standard in Yellow until after Rnd 16 then continue as follows:

Change to Charcoal

Rnd 17 dc

Change to Yellow

Rnd 18 (dc3, dc2tog) 6 times (24)

Rnd 19 dc

Rnd 20 dc3, (dc2tog) 9 times, dc3 (15)

Rnd 21 dc3, (dc2tog) 5 times, dc2 (10)

Rnd 22 dc

Rnd 23 (dc2 into next st) twice Yellow, (dc2 into next st) 3 times Ruby, (dc2 into next st) twice Yellow, (dc2 into next st) 3 times Ruby (20)

Stuff and continue

Rnd 24 dc3, dc2 into next st Yellow, dc3, dc2 into next st, dc2 Ruby, dc1, dc2 into next st, dc2 Yellow, dc1, dc2 into next st, dc3, dc2 into next st Ruby (25)

Rnd 25 dc2 into next st, dc4 Yellow, dc2 into next st, dc4, dc2 into next st, dc1 Ruby, dc3, dc2 into next st, dc1 Yellow, dc3, dc2 into next st, dc4 Ruby (30)

Rnd 26 (dc1 Yellow, dc1 Charcoal) 3 times, dc1 into same stitch Yellow, dc5, dc2 into next st, dc3 Ruby, dc2, dc2 into next st, dc4 Yellow, dc1, dc2 into next st, dc5, dc2 into next st Ruby (35)

Rnd 27 dc6, dc2 into next st Yellow, dc6, dc2 into next st, dc3 Ruby, dc3, dc2 into next st, dc5 Yellow, dc1, dc2 into next st, dc6, dc2 into next st Ruby (40)

Rnd 28 dc2 Yellow, dc1 Charcoal, dc2 Yellow, dc1 Charcoal, dc2 Yellow, dc11 Ruby, dc11 Yellow, dc10 Ruby

Rnd 29 dc8 Yellow, dc6 Ruby, dc20 Yellow, dc6 Ruby

Rnd 30 dc2tog Yellow, (dc1 Charcoal, dc1 Yellow) 3 times, dc2, dc2tog, dc2 Ruby, dc6, dc2tog, dc8, dc2tog, dc3 Yellow, dc5 Ruby (36)

Rnd 31 dc7 Yellow, dc3 Ruby, dc23 Yellow, dc3 Ruby

Continue in Yellow

Rnd 32 (dc4, dc2tog) 5 times, dc1, dc2tog, dc3 (30)

Rnd 33 (dc3, dc2tog) 6 times (24)

Rnd 34 (dc2, dc2tog) 6 times (18)

Rnd 35 dc

Rnd 36 (dc2tog) 9 times (9)

Stuff and gather remaining stitches to close.

LEGS (make two)

Work as standard PERCHING in Yellow changing to Coral after Rnd 5 working TIBIA as Rnds 1-3 dc (3 rnds) and TARSUS as Rnds 1-4 dc (4 rnds)

WINGS (make two)

Work as standard FLYING in Charcoal with colour pattern of dc2 Charcoal, dc1 Cream on every 3rd rnd throughout

BEAK

Working in Coral

Ch18 and sl st to join into a circle

Rnds 1-2 dc (2 rnds)

Rnd 3 dc2tog, dc16 (17)

Rnd 4 dc2tog, dc15 (16)

Rnd 5 dc2tog, dc14 (15)

Rnd 6 dc2tog, dc13 (14)

Rnd 7 dc2tog, dc12 (13)

Rnd 8 dc2tog, dc11 (12)

Rnd 9 dc

Rnd 10 dc2tog, dc10 (11)

Rnd 11 dc2tog, dc9 (10)

Rnd 12 dc2tog, dc8 (9)

Rnd 13 (dc1, dc2tog) 3 times (6)

Rnd 14 (dc1, dc2tog) twice (4)

Stuff lightly and sew into position.

CROWN

Working in Charcoal

Embroider stitches onto the top of the head to create a triangle shape.

CHEEKS

Working in Cream

Sl st into position on side of head, htr2 into same st and then htr2 into next st

Break yarn and repeat on other side of head.

TAIL

Working in Cream

Ch16 and sl st to join into a circle

Continue working 2 rnds Cream, 2 rnds Charcoal throughout

Rnds 1-6 dc (6 rnds)

Split into two rnds of 8 sts and work each as follows:

Rnds 1-4 dc (4 rnds)

Rnd 5 dc7, dc2 into next st (9)

Rnds 6-8 dc (3 rnds)

Rnd 9 dc8, dc2 into next st (10)

Rnds 10-12 dc (3 rnds)

Rnd 13 (dc4, dc2 into next st) twice (12)

Rnds 14-20 dc (7 rnds)

Continue in Charcoal

Rnd 21 (dc2, dc2tog) 3 times (9)

Rnd 22 (dc1, dc2tog) 3 times (6)

Rnd 23 (dc1, dc2tog) twice (4)

Break yarn.

Do not stuff. Sew flat across top to close.

Finish by sewing eyes into place with Black yarn.

AGATHA
the Vulturine Guinea Fowl

Agatha works very successfully in children's television despite having aways proclaimed that she doesn't really like them! She's always found kids (especially more than one at once) a little too much for her to handle, valuing calm and considered conversation over the undertone of bickering, smattering of whinging and constant questioning that often comes with a group of children. Perhaps it's her standoffish nature in combination with her stature that make her just so captivating to those young developing minds, although it could be her bold black and white stripes, comical beak, or maybe just that big fluffy body that looks great for a hug.

YARN REQUIRED

25g TOFT DK yarn Blue
25g TOFT DK yarn Charcoal
25g TOFT DK yarn Cream
25g TOFT DK yarn Shale
25g TOFT DK yarn Silver
25g TOFT DK yarn Chestnut
25g TOFT DK yarn Hyacinth

See also *You Will Need* and *Size Options*.

BODY/NECK/HEAD

Work as standard in Blue with 1.5cm (½in) LOOP STITCH every 4th st until after Rnd 23. Change to Shale and work NECK as Rnds 1-8 dc (8 rnds) then change to Chestnut and work HEAD changing to Hyacinth after Rnd 4

LEGS (make two)

Work as standard PERCHING in Charcoal changing to Shale after Rnd 5 working TIBIA as Rnds 1-2 dc (2 rnds) and TARSUS as Rnds 1-8 dc (8 rnds)

WINGS (make two)

Work as standard FLYING in Charcoal until after Rnd 6. Continue working spot pattern of dc2 Charcoal, dc1 Cream on every 3rd rnd throughout

Working in Cream

Embroider six stitches around the bottom of each wing by sewing from the starting ring and up to the round below the spots above.

Sew the wings into a downwards position on body.

BEAK

Working in Silver

Ch18 and sl st to join into a circle

Rnds 1-7 dc (7 rnds)

Rnd 8 dc3, (dc2tog) 6 times, dc3 (12)

Rnd 9 dc3, (dc2tog) 3 times, dc3 (9)

Rnd 10 dc2, (dc2tog) 3 times, dc1 (6)

Rnd 11 (dc2tog) 3 times (3)

Stuff lightly and sew into position.

NECK FEATHERS

Working in Cream

Sl st into colour change line at the side of the neck and then work five long feathers along the front of the neckline as follows:

*ch19 and sl st 18 back down chain, sl st 1 along neck

Repeat from * four times more, then work four short feathers along the back of the neck as follows:

*ch6 and sl st 5 back down chain, sl st 1 along neck

Break yarn.

Working in Charcoal

Work a line of sl st along the centre of each of the long front feathers. Hold the yarn on the underside of the feather for a neat finish on the top.

TAIL

Working in Charcoal

Begin by dc6 into ring

Rnd 1 (dc1, dc2 into next st) 3 times (9)

Rnd 2 dc

Rnd 3 (dc2, dc2 into next st) 3 times (12)

Rnd 4 dc

Rnd 5 (dc3, dc2 into next st) 3 times (15)

Rnd 6 dc

Rnd 7 (dc4, dc2 into next st) 3 times (18)

Rnd 8 (dc2 Charcoal, dc1 Cream) 6 times

Continue in Charcoal

Rnd 9 (dc5, dc2 into next st) 3 times (21)

Rnd 10 dc

Rnd 11 (dc2 Charcoal, dc1 Cream) 7 times

Continue in Charcoal

Rnd 12 (dc6, dc2 into next st) 3 times (24)

Rnd 13 dc

Change to Blue and work 1.5cm (½in) LOOP STITCH every 3rd st

Rnd 14 dc

Break yarn.

Do not stuff. Sew flat across top to close.

Working in Cream

Embroider five stitches around the bottom of the tail by sewing from the starting ring and up to the round below the spots above.

Finish by sewing eyes and nostrils into place with Black yarn.

RAEGAN
the King Penguin

With a taste for the finer things in life, Raegan had better hope he waddles his way into fame and fortune soon or he'll be having to swap caviar for fish fingers before the year is out. Head to toe in the latest designer outfits, this penguin certainly looks the part even if he's not yet learned the lines for his next role. Having fallen in love with lights, camera and action only last year, he's hopeful that this next one will be his big-break part that has him swimming into the spotlight. As this latest director shouts 'ready on set' Raegan knows he's ready for anything and hungry for that starring role he's been dreaming of.

YARN REQUIRED

25g TOFT DK yarn Cream
25g TOFT DK yarn Yellow
25g TOFT DK yarn Charcoal
25g TOFT DK yarn Steel

See also *You Will Need* and *Size Options*.

BODY/NECK/HEAD

Working in Cream

Begin by dc6 into ring

Rnd 1 (dc2 into next st) 6 times (12)

Rnd 2 (dc1, dc2 into next st) 6 times (18)

Rnd 3 (dc2, dc2 into next st) 6 times (24)

Rnd 4 (dc3, dc2 into next st) 6 times (30)

Rnd 5 (dc4, dc2 into next st) 6 times (36)

Rnd 6 (dc5, dc2 into next st) 6 times (42)

Rnds 7-8 dc21 Steel, dc21 Cream (2 rnds)

Rnd 9 dc1 Cream, dc20 Steel, dc21 Cream

Rnd 10 dc1 Cream, dc4, dc2tog, (dc5, dc2tog) twice Steel, (dc5, dc2tog) 3 times Cream (36)

Rnds 11-13 dc2 Cream, dc16 Steel, dc18 Cream (3 rnds)

Rnd 14 dc3 Cream, dc15 Steel, dc18 Cream

Rnd 15 dc3 Cream, dc1, dc2tog, (dc4, dc2tog) twice Steel, (dc4, dc2tog) 3 times Cream (30)

Rnd 16 dc3 Cream, dc12 Steel, dc15 Cream

Rnds 17-18 dc4 Cream, dc11 Steel, dc15 Cream (2 rnds)

Rnd 19 dc5 Cream, dc10 Steel, dc15 Cream

Rnd 20 dc3, dc2tog Cream, (dc3, dc2tog) twice Steel, (dc3, dc2tog) 3 times Yellow (24)

Rnd 21 dc5 Yellow, dc7 Steel, dc12 Yellow

Next dc6 Yellow, move st marker to this point for new end of round

Rnd 22 dc6 Steel, (dc2tog) 9 times Yellow (15)

Rnd 23 dc2tog, dc4 Steel, (dc2tog) 4 times, dc1 Yellow (10)

Stuff and continue

Rnd 24 dc5 Steel, dc5 Yellow

Next dc5 Steel

RESET Rnd

Rnd 25 (dc2 into next st) 6 times Yellow, (dc2 into next st) 4 times Steel (20)

Rnd 26 (dc3, dc2 into next st) 3 times Yellow, (dc3, dc2 into next st) twice Charcoal (25)

Rnd 27 (dc4, dc2 into next st) 3 times Yellow, (dc4, dc2 into next st) twice Charcoal (30)

Rnd 28 (dc2, dc2 into next st) 6 times Yellow, (dc2, dc2 into next st) 4 times Charcoal (40)

Rnd 29 dc24 Yellow, dc16 Charcoal

Continue in Charcoal

Rnds 30-31 dc (2 rnds)

Rnd 32 (dc8, dc2tog) 4 times (36)

Rnd 33 dc

Rnd 34 (dc4, dc2tog) 6 times (30)

Rnd 35 (dc3, dc2tog) 6 times (24)

Rnd 36 (dc2, dc2tog) 6 times (18)

Rnd 37 dc

Rnd 38 (dc2tog) 9 times (9)

Stuff and gather remaining stitches to close.

LEGS

Working in Cream

Ch30 and sl st to join into a circle

Rnds 1-4 dc (4 rnds)

Split into two rnds of 15 sts and work each as follows:

Rnd 1 dc

Rnd 2 dc13, dc2tog (14)

Rnd 3 dc12, dc2tog (13)

Rnd 4 dc11, dc2tog (12)

Rnd 5 (dc4, dc2tog) twice (10)

Change to Charcoal

Rnd 6 (dc3, dc2tog) twice (8)

Rnd 7 dc

Rnd 8 (dc2, dc2tog) twice (6)

Rnd 9 (dc2 into next st) 6 times (12)

Rnd 10 (dc1, dc2 into next st) 6 times (18)

Rnds 11-16 dc (6 rnds)

Split into three rnds of 6 sts and work each as follows:

Rnds 1-2 dc (2 rnds)

Rnd 3 dc

Rnd 4 (dc2tog) 3 times (3)

Break yarn.

Stuff the top of the legs and sew the open top into position around the bottom of the body. Fold the ankles forwards and sew to secure.

WING ONE

Working in Steel

Begin by dc6 into ring

Rnd 1 dc2, dc2 into next st Steel, dc2 into next st Cream, dc2 Steel (8)

Rnd 2 dc3, dc2 into next st Steel, dc2 into next st, dc1 Cream, dc2 Steel (10)

Rnd 3 dc4, dc2 into next st Steel, dc2 into next st, dc2 Cream, dc2 Steel (12)

Rnd 4 dc5, dc2 into next st Steel, dc2 into next st, dc3 Cream, dc2 Steel (14)

Rnd 5 dc6, dc2 into next st Steel, dc2 into next st, dc4 Cream, dc2 Steel (16)

Rnd 6 dc7, dc2 into next st Steel, dc2 into next st, dc5 Cream, dc2 Steel (18)

Rnd 7 dc8, dc2 into next st Steel, dc2 into next st, dc6 Cream, dc2 Steel (20)

Rnds 8-12 dc10 Steel, dc8 Cream, dc2 Steel (5 rnds)

Rnds 13-17 dc11 Steel, dc7 Cream, dc2 Steel (5 rnds)

Rnd 18 dc1, (dc2tog) twice, dc6 Steel, dc4, (dc2tog) twice Cream, dc1 Steel (16)

Rnd 19 dc1, (dc2tog) twice, dc4 Steel, dc2, (dc2tog) twice Cream, dc1 Steel (12)

Rnd 20 dc Steel

Do not stuff.

WING TWO

Working in Steel

Begin by dc6 into ring

Rnd 1 dc1 Cream, dc1, (dc2 into next st) twice, dc2 Steel (8)

Rnd 2 dc2 Cream, dc1, (dc2 into next st) twice, dc3 Steel (10)

Rnd 3 dc3 Cream, dc1, (dc2 into next st) twice, dc4 Steel (12)

Rnd 4 dc4 Cream, dc1, (dc2 into next st) twice, dc5 Steel (14)

Rnd 5 dc5 Cream, dc1, (dc2 into next st) twice, dc6 Steel (16)

Rnd 6 dc6 Cream, dc1, (dc2 into next st) twice, dc7 Steel (18)

Rnd 7 dc7 Cream, dc1, (dc2 into next st) twice, dc8 Steel (20)

Rnd 8 dc8 Cream, dc12 Steel

Rnds 9-12 dc9 Cream, dc11 Steel (4 rnds)

Rnds 13-17 dc1 Steel, dc8 Cream, dc11 Steel (5 rnds)

Rnd 18 dc1 Steel, (dc2tog) twice, dc4 Cream, dc6, (dc2tog) twice, dc1 Steel (16)

Rnd 19 dc1 Steel, (dc2tog) twice, dc2 Cream, dc4, (dc2tog) twice, dc1 Steel (12)

Rnd 20 dc Steel

Do not stuff.

BEAK

Working in Charcoal

Begin by dc4 into ring

Rnds 1-2 dc (2 rnds)

Rnd 3 dc2 into next st, dc3 (5)

Rnd 4 dc2 into next st, dc4 (6)

Rnd 5 dc2 into next st, dc5 (7)

Rnd 6 dc2 into next st, dc6 (8)

Rnd 7 dc2 into next st, dc7 (9)

Rnd 8 dc2 into next st, dc8 (10)

Rnd 9 dc2 into next st, dc9 (11)

Rnd 10 dc2 into next st, dc10 (12)

Rnd 11 (dc2 into next st, dc3) 3 times (15)

Rnd 12 dc

Stuff lightly and sew into position.

Working in Yellow

Embroider stitches onto either side of the beak.

TAIL

Working in Steel

Ch24 and sl st to join into a circle

Rnds 1-4 dc (4 rnds)

Rnd 5 (dc2tog) 12 times (12)

Rnd 6 dc

Rnd 7 (dc2tog) 6 times (6)

Break yarn.

Do not stuff. Sew flat across top to close.

Finish by sewing eyes into place with Black yarn.

CALLAHAN
the Yokohama Cockerel

Callahan is the best looking cockerel in the coop (and he knows it). An online life-coach that's making a good living bringing out the best in others, Callahan's cup has always been half-full, and now he spends every day showing others how to make sure theirs is too. Exactly the kind of bird you'll want to have cheering you on from the sidelines, a few hours in his company and you'll be jumping out of bed to the sound of his cock-a-doodle-do the next morning. Equipped with his secret weapons of a good comb, some hairwax and a pocket mirror, before too long he'll have taught you how to embrace that every single moment in life is an opportunity to shake your tail feathers.

YARN REQUIRED

25g TOFT DK yarn Charcoal
25g TOFT DK yarn Chestnut
25g TOFT DK yarn Camel
25g TOFT DK yarn Cream
25g TOFT DK yarn Oatmeal
25g TOFT DK yarn Shale
25g TOFT DK yarn Silver
25g TOFT DK yarn Fudge
25g TOFT DK yarn Ruby
25g TOFT DK yarn Teal

See also *You Will Need* and *Size Options*.

BODY/HEAD

Working in Charcoal

Begin by dc6 into ring

Rnd 1 (dc2 into next st) 6 times (12)

Rnd 2 (dc1, dc2 into next st) 6 times (18)

Rnd 3 (dc2, dc2 into next st) 6 times (24)

Rnd 4 (dc3, dc2 into next st) 6 times (30)

Rnd 5 (dc4, dc2 into next st) 6 times (36)

Rnd 6 (dc5, dc2 into next st) 6 times (42)

Rnds 7-9 dc (3 rnds)

Rnd 10 (dc5, dc2tog) 6 times (36)

Rnds 11-12 dc (2 rnds)

Change to Chestnut

Rnds 13-14 dc (2 rnds)

Rnd 15 (dc4, dc2tog) 6 times (30)

Rnds 16-17 (2 rnds)

Change to Camel

Rnds 18-19 dc (2 rnds)

Rnd 20 (dc3, dc2tog) 6 times (24)

Rnd 21 dc

Rnd 22 dc3, (dc2tog) 9 times, dc3 (15)

Rnd 23 dc3, (dc2tog) 5 times, dc2 (10)

Stuff and continue

Rnd 24 dc

Rnd 25 (dc2 into next st) 3 times Camel, (dc2 into next st) 5 times Ruby, (dc2 into next st) twice Camel (20)

Rnd 26 dc3, dc2 into next st, dc2 Camel, dc1, dc2 into next st, (dc3, dc2 into next st) twice Ruby, dc3, dc2 into next st Camel (25)

Rnd 27 dc4, dc2 into next st, dc2 Camel, dc2, dc2 into next st, (dc4, dc2 into next st) twice Ruby, dc4, dc2 into next st Camel (30)

Rnd 28 (dc2, dc2 into next st) twice, dc2 Camel, dc2 into next st, (dc2, dc2 into next st) 5 times Cream, (dc2, dc2 into next st) twice Camel (40)

Rnds 29-31 dc10 Camel, dc22 Cream, dc8 Camel (3 rnds)

Rnd 32 dc8, dc2tog, dc1 Camel, dc7, dc2tog, dc8, dc2tog, dc3 Cream, dc5, dc2tog Camel (36)

Rnd 33 dc10 Camel, dc20 Cream, dc6 Camel

Rnd 34 dc4, dc2tog, dc4 Camel, dc2tog, (dc4, dc2tog) 3 times Cream, dc4, dc2tog Camel (30)

Rnd 35 dc3, dc2tog, dc4 Camel, dc2tog, dc2, dc2tog (dc3, dc2tog) twice Cream, dc3, dc2tog Camel (24)

Continue in Camel

Rnd 36 (dc2, dc2tog) 6 times (18)

Rnd 37 dc

Rnd 38 (dc2tog) 9 times (9)

Stuff and gather remaining stitches to close.

LEGS (make two)

Work as standard PERCHING in Charcoal changing to Shale after Rnd 5 working TIBIA as Rnds 1-7 dc (7 rnds) and TARSUS as Rnds 1-8 dc (8 rnds)

WINGS (make two)

Working in Chestnut

Begin by dc6 into ring

Rnd 1 (dc1, dc2 into next st) 3 times (9)

Rnd 2 dc8, dc2 into next st (10)

Rnd 3 dc

Rnd 4 dc9, dc2 into next st (11)

Rnd 5 dc

Rnd 6 dc10, dc2 into next st (12)

Rnd 7 dc

Rnd 8 dc11, dc2 into next st (13)

Rnd 9 dc

Rnd 10 dc12, dc2 into next st (14)

Change to Teal

Rnd 11 dc

Rnd 12 (dc6, dc2 into next st) twice (16)

Rnd 13 dc2 into next st, dc14, dc2 into next st (18)

Rnd 14 dc2 into next st, dc16, dc2 into next st (20)

Rnd 15 dc2 into next st, dc18, dc2 into next st (22)

Rnd 16 dc2 into next st, dc20, dc2 into next st (24)

Rnd 17 dc2 into next st, dc22, dc2 into next st (26)

Rnds 18-21 dc (4 rnds)

Rnd 22 (dc11, dc2tog) twice (24)

Rnd 23 (dc2, dc2tog) 6 times (18)

Rnd 24 dc

Rnd 25 (dc1, dc2tog) 6 times (12)

Rnd 26 (dc2tog) 6 times (6)

Break yarn, gather stitches. Do not stuff.

BEAK

Working in Silver

Ch12 and sl st to join into a circle

Rnd 1 dc

Rnd 2 (dc2, dc2tog) 3 times (9)

Rnd 3 dc

Rnd 4 dc2tog, dc7 (8)

Rnd 5 dc2tog, dc6 (7)

Rnd 6 dc2tog, dc5 (6)

Rnd 7 dc2tog, dc4 (5)

Stuff lightly and sew into position.

CREST

Working in Ruby

Ch36 and sl st to join into a circle

Rnds 1-2 dc (2 rnds)

Rnd 3 dc6 (incomplete rnd)

Count 6 sts backwards, split and work these sts as follows:

Rnds 1-2 dc (2 rnds)

Rnd 3 dc4, dc2tog (5)

Rnd 4 dc3, dc2tog (4)

Break yarn.

Rejoin and work next 8-st rnd (4 sts each side) as follows:

Rnds 1-2 dc (2 rnds)

Rnd 3 dc6, dc2tog (7)

Rnd 4 dc5, dc2tog (6)

Rnd 5 dc4, dc2tog (5)

Rnd 6 dc3, dc2tog (4)

Break yarn.

Rejoin and work next 10-st rnd (5 sts each side) as follows:

Rnds 1-2 dc (2 rnds)

Rnd 3 dc8, dc2tog (9)

Rnd 4 dc7, dc2tog (8)

Rnd 5 dc6, dc2tog (7)

Rnd 6 dc5, dc2tog (6)

Rnd 7 dc4, dc2tog (5)

Rnd 8 dc3, dc2tog (4)

Break yarn.

Rejoin and work last 12-st rnd as follows:

Rnds 1-2 dc (2 rnds)

Rnd 3 dc10, dc2tog (11)

Rnd 4 dc9, dc2tog (10)

Rnd 5 dc8, dc2tog (9)

Rnd 6 dc7, dc2tog (8)

Rnd 7 dc6, dc2tog (7)

Rnd 8 dc5, dc2tog (6)

Rnd 9 dc4, dc2tog (5)

Rnd 10 dc3, dc2tog (4)

Break yarn.

Stuff lightly and sew into position on top of head, with the shortest prong at the front.

Working in Ruby, embroider stitches onto the head between the crest and the beak.

WATTLE (make two)

Working in Ruby

Begin by dc6 into ring

Rnd 1 (dc2 into next st) 6 times (12)

Rnd 2 (dc1, dc2 into next st) 6 times (18)

Rnds 3-5 dc (3 rnds)

Rnd 6 (dc4, dc2tog) 3 times (15)

Rnd 7 (dc3, dc2tog) 3 times (12)

Rnd 8 dc

Rnd 9 (dc1, dc2tog) 4 times (8)

Rnd 10 (dc1, dc2 into the next st) 4 times (12)

Do not stuff.

Sew into position underneath chin.

COLLAR

Working in Camel and working from the bottom upwards

*Sl st into position at neck, ch9 and work back down chain as follows:

Sl st 2, dc2, htr2, tr2

Repeat from * around the neck to make five feathers.

Working in Fudge

*Sl st into position underneath the round of Camel feathers, ch13 and work back down chain as follows:

Sl st 3, dc3, htr3, tr3

Rep from * around the neck to make eight feathers.

TAIL

BOTTOM FEATHERS

Working in Charcoal and working from the bottom upwards

*Sl st into tail position at the side of the body, ch25 and work back down chain as follows:

Sl st 4, dc4, htr4, tr12

Repeat from * to make a row of four feathers.

Work another row of four Charcoal feathers above the previous row.

MIDDLE FEATHERS

Working in Charcoal

*Sl st above the previous row, ch29 and work back down chain as follows:

Sl st 4, dc4, htr4, tr16

Repeat from * to make a row of three feathers.

Work another row of three Oatmeal feathers above the previous row.

TOP FEATHERS

Working in Camel

*Sl st above the previous row, ch29 and work back down chain as follows:

Sl st 4, dc 4, htr4, tr16

Repeat from * once more to make a row of two feathers.

Finish by sewing eyes into place with Black yarn.

TECHNICALS

In the following pages I aim to equip a complete beginner with the skills to make any or all of these birds. Even if you are a seasoned crocheter, take the time to glance over the instructions as specific techniques to this style of crochet, such as decreasing and colour changing, may be new to you and will be essential to get right on those smaller rounds with fewer stitches.

BASIC SKILLS

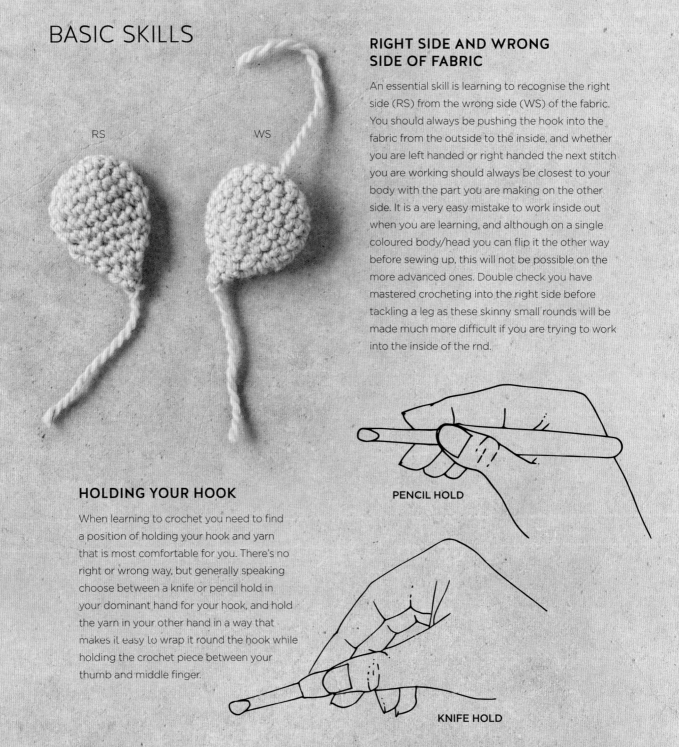

RS   WS

RIGHT SIDE AND WRONG SIDE OF FABRIC

An essential skill is learning to recognise the right side (RS) from the wrong side (WS) of the fabric. You should always be pushing the hook into the fabric from the outside to the inside, and whether you are left handed or right handed the next stitch you are working should always be closest to your body with the part you are making on the other side. It is a very easy mistake to work inside out when you are learning, and although on a single coloured body/head you can flip it the other way before sewing up, this will not be possible on the more advanced ones. Double check you have mastered crocheting into the right side before tackling a leg as these skinny small rounds will be made much more difficult if you are trying to work into the inside of the rnd.

PENCIL HOLD

HOLDING YOUR HOOK

When learning to crochet you need to find a position of holding your hook and yarn that is most comfortable for you. There's no right or wrong way, but generally speaking choose between a knife or pencil hold in your dominant hand for your hook, and hold the yarn in your other hand in a way that makes it easy to wrap it round the hook while holding the crochet piece between your thumb and middle finger.

KNIFE HOLD

SPLITTING ROUNDS

To avoid the birds being made of lots of small pieces that you have to sew together at the end, the legs and tails all call for you to 'split the rnd' into smaller rounds. To ensure that these smaller rounds sit flat alongside each other the stitches are divided as in the following example (perching leg). Count backwards to split the first six stitches and work a toe, then the next toe of six stitches will be worked half from the top 3 sts and half from the bottom 3 sts of the main round, then the third toe will be worked from the final six stitches that remain. See *Working the Stitches* for steps.

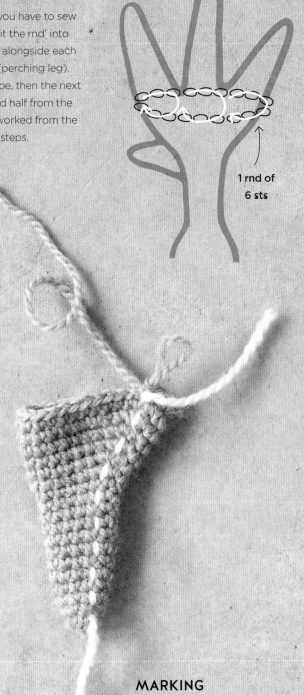

1 rnd of
6 sts

ABBREVIATIONS

ch: Chain. A chain is the most fundamental of all crochet stitches.

dc: Double crochet. Using the double crochet stitch creates a compact and dense fabric. (NB: this is known as sc – single crochet – in US terminology.)

dc2tog: Double crochet two stitches together decrease by one stitch).

Rnd: Round. A round is a complete rotation in a spiral back to your stitch marker. With these patterns you DO NOT slip stitch at the end of a round to make a circle, but instead continue straight onto the next round in a spiral.

Row: Rows create a flat piece of fabric rather than working in a spiral. When working a row turn and work immediately back into the stitch you've just worked to keep the same number of stitches on each row.

RS: Right side. The right side of your fabric will show small 'V' shapes in horizontal lines and will form the outside of the animal.

RESET Rnd: Move your stitch marker to this place and begin the next rnd of instruction from here regardless of whether the last rnd was completed.

sl st: Slip stitch. This is the simplest crochet stitch.

st(s): Stitch(es). You can count your stitches around the edge of your fabric.

htr: Half treble. A step-up from the dc with an extra wrap of yarn (known as hdc in US terminology).

tr: Treble. A longer more open stitch than the double crochet (known as dc – double crochet – in US terminology).

dtr: Double Treble. A very long stitch with one more repeated step to the treble (known as tr – triple crochet – in US terminology.

MB: Make a bobble.

WS: Wrong side. The wrong side of your fabric will have vertical spiralling furrows. This is where you have all the ends or strands of yarn, and it forms the inside of the animal.

MARKING

Use a stitch marker to keep track of the end of each round as you work. I recommend tying in a piece of contrast yarn approximately 15cm (6in) long after the end of Rnd 1 as you get back around to it, pull it forwards or backwards over your stitches to weave a marker up your fabric. The marker can be removed when finished.

WORKING THE STITCHES

SLIP KNOT

1. Make a loop in the yarn.

2. Pull the yarn through the loop.

3. Place your hook through the loop and tighten.

CHAIN

1. With your slip knot on your hook, wrap yarn over the hook (yarn over).

2. Twist the hook downwards and pull the yarn through the loop.

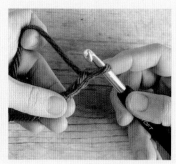

3. Repeat until desired length.

SLIP STITCH TO JOIN INTO CIRCLE

1. Chain the number of stitches stated, then insert the hook into the stitch closest to the slip knot.

2. Yarn over hook, pull the yarn through the stitch and loop on the hook in one motion.

3. Work the first stitch of the round into the last chain that you made.

NB: US crocheters will know this stitch as single crochet (sc).

1. Insert the hook through the stitch under both loops of the 'V'.

2. Yarn over and pull through the stitch (two loops on hook).

3. Yarn over again and pull through both loops to end with one loop.

1. Make a slip knot and chain two stitches, then insert the hook into the first chain stitch.

2. Work a double crochet stitch into this stitch.

3. Work five more double crochet stitches into this same stitch to make six stitches in total. Pull tightly on the tail of the yarn to close the centre of the ring and form a neat circle.

1. Insert the hook through the front loop of the stitch only (two loops on the hook).

2. Insert the hook through the front loop of the next stitch (three loops on the hook).

3. Yarn over hook and pull through first two loops on the hook, then yarn over and through both remaining loops to complete the double crochet.

NB: On a rnd with more than one colour the colour the stitches should be worked in always follows the instruction.

CHANGING COLOUR

1. On your last stitch before the colour change. Insert the hook through the next stitch, yarn over and pull through the stitch (two loops on hook).

2. Yarn over with the new colour and complete the double crochet stitch with this new yarn.

3. Continue with this new colour, leaving the original colour to the back of the work. Cut if a one-off colour change or run on the WS of the fabric if colour changing back to it.

SPLITTING ROUNDS

1. Count the number of stitches in new smaller round back from your hook.

2. Cross the round to double crochet into this stitch on the right side of the fabric.

3. Once you have completed this smaller round, break yarn and rejoin to work the next small round. See *Basic Skills*.

WORKING ROWS

1. Chain the number of stitches stated in the pattern.

2. Starting in the second chain from hook, work back along these chain stitches to create the first row.

3. Turn piece so that the back of the previous row is facing you. Start in the first stitch next to your hook and work the next row along the row of stitches.

CHAIN SPLIT

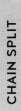   

1. Chain 6 stitches.

2. Miss 2 stitches from main round and sl st into third stitch.

3. Dc2 along the two remaining stitches from main round and then dc6 along the chain to create an 8-stitch round.

134

NB: For htr, work as tr step 1 and then at step 3 yarn over and pull through all loops.
For dtr, yarn over twice during step 1 and then repeat step 2 before step 3.

1. Yarn over and insert the hook into the stitch.

2. Yarn over and pull through the stitch (three loops on hook), yarn over and pull through first two loops on hook.

3. Yarn over and pull through remaining two loops on hook.

1. Insert the hook through the stitch, wrap the yarn from front to back around your thumb, yarn over and pull through the stitch.

2. Pull the loop to the front and to length stated in the pattern, then yarn over and pull through the two loops on hook to complete the stitch.

3. Repeat to work loops as often as stated in the pattern. Measure loops from the fabric to the end of the loop.

1. Yarn over and insert hook into stitch, yarn over and bring through the stitch.

2. Yarn over and bring through the first two loops. Repeat steps 1-2 once more.

3. Yarn over, insert hook into stitch, yarn over and bring through the stitch, then yarn over and bring through all loops on hook.

FINISHING TECHNIQUES

These techniques are worked onto the surface of the bird once it has been stuffed and sewn up.

SLIP STITCH TRAVERSE IN A RING

1. Insert the hook into the fabric around a stitch and yarn over.

2. Pull through the fabric and loop in one motion.

3. Continue moving around the fabric like this to create a ring into which you will work the first round of stitches.

CHAIN LOOPS

1. Insert the hook into the fabric around a stitch, yarn over and pull through the fabric.

2. Chain the number of stitches stated in the pattern, then insert hook into the fabric approx. two stitches and two rows away. Yarn over and pull through the fabric.

3. Repeat step 2 until the area is covered.

SLIP STITCH CHAINS

1. Insert the hook into the fabric around a stitch, yarn over and pull through the fabric.

2. Chain the number of stitches stated in the pattern.

3. Slip stitch back down the chain and then slip stitch into the fabric. Repeat as instructed.

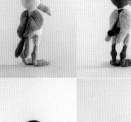

MAKE YOUR TAIL FEATHERS

Consider the character of your bird before positioning the wings and tail.

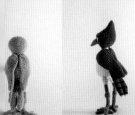

STUFFING AND SEWING

When stuffing your bird remember that you want to show off its shape, but don't want to make it too firm and hard. Much of the appeal with this collection comes from the drape of the limbs, which is created through a combination of the luxury yarn and light-handed stuffing. Once you have crocheted the pieces and pushed the stuffing into them, you will need to roll and manipulate the pieces in your hands to spread the stuffing evenly and ensure the best shape.

STUFFING THE BODY/NECK/HEAD

All the bodies, necks and heads are stuffed in one piece. To avoid creating a floppy-headed bird ensure you view this piece as one, and get a continuous piece of stuffing running from the body through the neck and up into the head rather than there being a break in stuffing in the neck.

STUFFING THE LEGS AND FINISHING THE FEET

While it is not essential to stuff the legs at all on the birds, on some patterns I will recommend a small pinch of stuffing into the bottom of the toes, feet or thighs to give a bit more shape. In order to aid the birds to sit up on your mantelpiece, nursery shelf or dashboard you need to splay the legs and sew them on the lines that divide the bottom into thirds (see *Sewing on Legs and Tail*).

DO NOT STUFF THE WINGS AND TAILS

Wings and tails are sewn onto your bird without stuffing. For wings gather the remaining stitch in the round and for tails sew them flat before sewing into place.

SEWING IN ENDS

When sewing in ends simply thread onto a wool needle and follow the instruction to either gather any remaining stitches on the round or sew flat to close before securing through the piece. It will be much eaiser to get a neat finish when sewing up if you leave at least a 10cm (4in) length whenever you break yarn.

OVERSEWING

Whenever you are sewing two pieces together that are the same colour you can use a simple oversewing technique between the piece and through the body down the flat edge of the piece. On most legs and tails that are a contrasting colour to the body I have added colour changing following a starting chain to make it easier to neatly sew them into position. This means you can sew them flat and then oversew between both sides of the piece and the body to make them very secure.

BACK STITCHING

Back stitching is the best method for attaching a contrasting colour piece onto the body such as a wing or beak once the body is stuffed.

1. Sew into the fabric down through an edge stitch and into the body/head fabric

2. Bring the needle up through both fabrics two stitches along the edge you are sewing

3. Sew back down one stitch behind this before repeating right around the edge.

Top

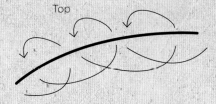

ORDER OF SEWING

1. Line up your chest shaping using centraliser marker and back stitch your wings into position either side of body at the desired angle as diagram.

2. Oversew your legs into position as diagram.

3. Oversew the tail horizontally at the back between the wings.

4. Position the beak in the centre of the head equally spaced above both wings and back stitch into place.

5. Sew the eyes into place and complete with any additional details.

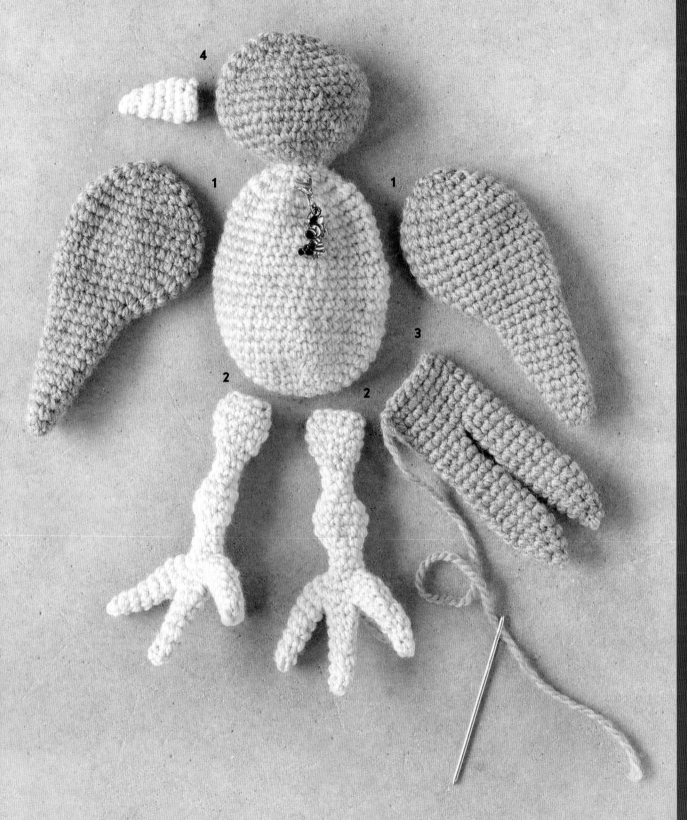

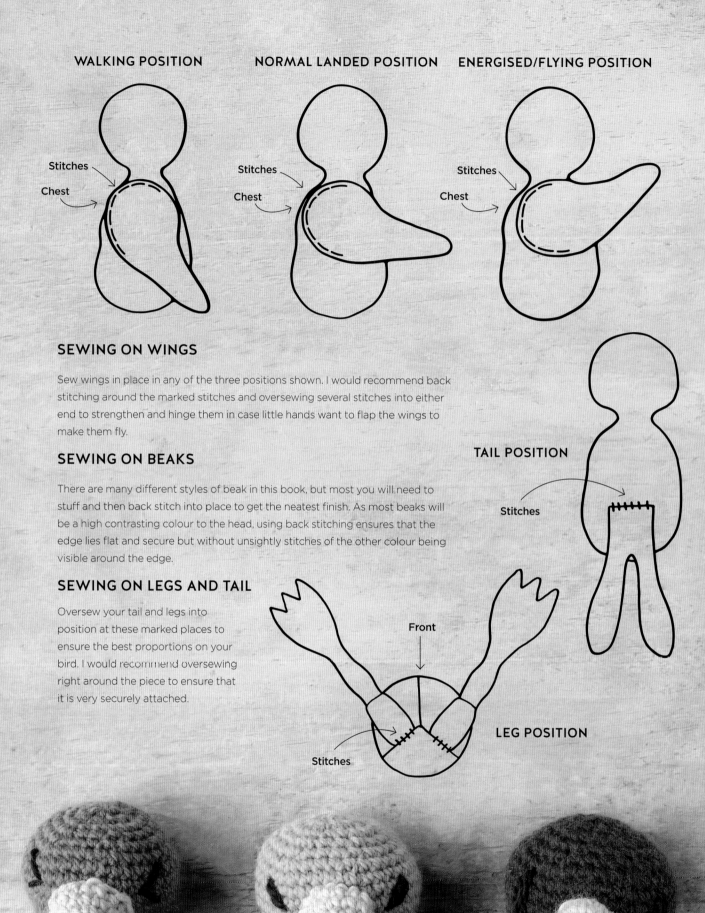

WALKING POSITION

Stitches

Chest

NORMAL LANDED POSITION

Stitches

Chest

ENERGISED/FLYING POSITION

Stitches

Chest

SEWING ON WINGS

Sew wings in place in any of the three positions shown. I would recommend back stitching around the marked stitches and oversewing several stitches into either end to strengthen and hinge them in case little hands want to flap the wings to make them fly.

SEWING ON BEAKS

There are many different styles of beak in this book, but most you will need to stuff and then back stitch into place to get the neatest finish. As most beaks will be a high contrasting colour to the head, using back stitching ensures that the edge lies flat and secure but without unsightly stitches of the other colour being visible around the edge.

SEWING ON LEGS AND TAIL

Oversew your tail and legs into position at these marked places to ensure the best proportions on your bird. I would recommend oversewing right around the piece to ensure that it is very securely attached.

TAIL POSITION

Stitches

Front

Stitches

LEG POSITION

SEWING ON EYES / EMBROIDERY

When sewing the eyes I have used a simple method of two wraps of yarn running vertically through the same stitches across three rows (see Ernest the Canary in Yellow on the far right below).

Sewing on the face details is when your bird's personality really begins to emerge. Take your time to get this right and don't be afraid to cut it all off and start again as many times as you need to and experiment with the style you like. Use the same method of basic embroidery for all details.

ADDING MODELLING WIRE

If you wish your birds to stand up then you can add a soft modelling wire to their legs. This is done most easily by stuffing and sewing your whole bird and then inserting a length of wire up one leg, turn it back down inside the body and then back down the other leg in one piece. Wings can also be wired if desired. Wire should be only used for birds that are for display well out of the reach of all children.

WIRE POSITION

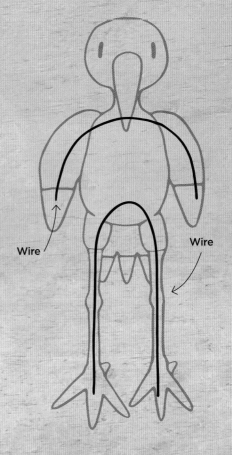

Wire   Wire

WASHING

If made in natural yarn and stuffed with synthetic stuffing material, the birds can either be washed by hand or on a gentle cold machine cycle. Please be aware that if you opt to use natural stuffing sponge the surface clean for the best results.

SAFETY

Your bird will only be as safe as you make it, so don't skimp on the stitches when sewing up. With ears and legs, I oversew all the way around the edges – you really can't sew them too much! I have also only used yarn to sew on eyes. You could use beads or buttons as an alternative. Never use toy safety eyes, beads or buttons on an animal intended for a child under three years old; you should embroider the details instead.

THANK YOU

These bright bird patterns have been remade and tested so many times by so many hands in the last decade that it's impossible to list all those people here.

For the creation of this new edition of the book I would like to give specific thanks to TOFT team members Natasha Jackson for her speedy hook in making very many knobbly knees and Rachel Critchley for her sharp attention to detail on absorbing everything I've learned over the last ten years. This book would not look anywhere near as beautiful without the incredible talent and skills of the TOFT creative team, Rosie Collins, Beth Plumbley and Yantra Taneva.

Wider thanks are due to the TOFT team past and present who work hard every day to delivery TOFT products around the world and help our customers learn to crochet and enjoy the craft as much as we do. Working alongside a group of such creative and dedicated people is an honour.

Without the support of my family I could not continue to run an expanding business. Thank you to Farah, Edward and Alex for being ever-tolerant of finding wool needles in the sofa and never tiring of snipping off ends. The honest feedback I get from you three is always inspiring, and it's that which spurs me on to keep creating every day.

Thank you to David and Charles for letting me revisit this special book a decade on from its first publication and divulge everything I have learned teaching people to crochet in that time.

A final thanks to all the *Edward's Menagerie* fans out there who continue to support TOFT. Your passion for my designs and our yarns keeps me crocheting as fast as I can!

SUPPLIERS

All the animals in the *Edward's Menagerie* collection of mammals and birds are made using TOFT yarns in fine, double knitting, aran and chunky weights. With the publication of this new edition of *Edward's Menagerie: Birds* TOFT now manufactures 36 shades of pure wool double knitting yarn. Only the highest-quality natural fibres are selected for use in TOFT yarns to ensure they are a pleasure to work with and will guarantee a stunning look and feel in your completed project.

For how-to videos and to purchase TOFT yarns to accompany this book visit:

www.toftuk.com

To find international stockists of TOFT yarns and kits see the website for details.

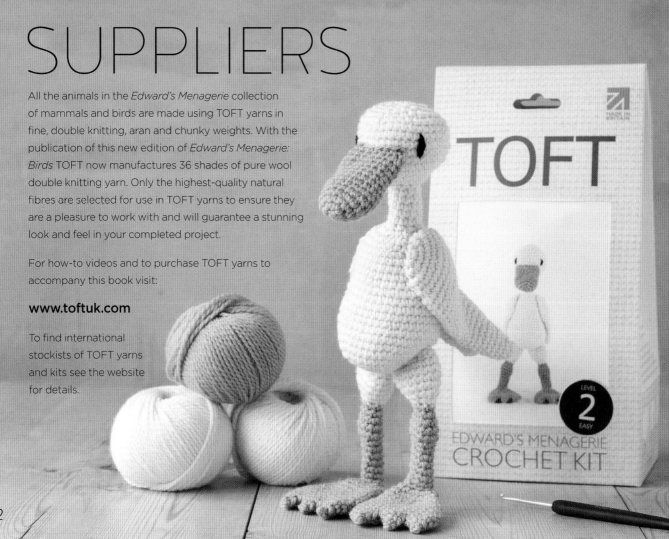

INDEX

abbreviations 131

back stitching 138
Bald Eagle, Abraham the 78–9
Barn Owl, Barney the 42–3
beaks 140
Birds of Paradise (Lesser), Putu the 104–5
Blue Tit, Desmond the 38–9
Blue-Footed Booby, Vince the 32–3
Blue-Winged Teal, Arthur the 60–1
bobbles 135
bodies 15, 138
Budgerigar, Terence the 110–11

Canary, Ernest the 22–3
Cassoway, Kevin the 80–1
chain loops 136
chain split 134
chain stitch 132
chickens
    Callahan the Yokohama Cockerel 126–9
    Hazel the Hen 58–9
    Tricia the Silkie Chicken 84–5
Cockatiel, Yolanda the 100–1
Cockatoo, Elvis the 88–9
Cockerel, Callahan the Yokohama 126–9
colour changes 134
counting stitches 14
Crane, Zane the Grey Crowned 76–7

decrease (DC2TOG) 133
Dodo, Elizabeth the 68–9
double crochet stitch 133
Dove, Celine the 28–9

Eagle, Abraham the Bald 78–9
embroidery 141

equipment 10
eyes 10, 141

fabric, right/wrong side of 130
faces 10, 141
feet 16, 18, 138
Finch, Ezra the Gouldian 114–15
finishing techniques 136
Flamingo, Sophia the 30–1
foundation ring (DC6 into ring) 133

Gouldian Finch, Ezra the 114–15
Grey Crowned Crane, Zane the 76–7
Guinea Fowl, Agatha the Vulturine 120–1
Gull, Dave the 24–5

heads 15, 138
Hen, Hazel the 58–9
holding techniques 130
hooks
    holding techniques 130
    sizes 12–13
Hoopoe, Jacob the 48–9

Jay, Jorge the 94–5

King Penguin, Raegan the 122–5
Kingfisher, Ben the 98–9
Kiwi, Ethel the 46–7

legs 16–18, 138, 140
    climbing 18
    grasping 16, 18
    paddling 16–17
    perching 16–17, 20
    swimming 16–17
Lesser Bird of Paradise, Putu the 104–5
Level 1 birds 8, 20–49
Level 2 birds 8, 50–85

Level 3 birds 8, 12, 86–129
Long-Eared Owl, Enid the 112–13
loop stitch 135
Lovebird, Gianni the 102–3

Macaw, Jack the 106–7
Magpie, Alan the 40–1
make bobble (MD) 135
Mallard, Duke the 26–7
marking 131
modelling wire 141

necks 15, 138
Northern Cardinal, Rory the 54–5

Ostrich, Florian the 70–1
oversewing 138
owls
    Barney the Barn Owl 42–3
    Enid the Long-Eared Owl 112–13

Peacock, Rohit the 116–17
Pelican, Huck the 44–5
Penguin, Raegan the King 122–5
Pink Robin, Travis the 82–3
Puffin, Gareth the 96–7

Raven, Henry the 52–3
Red Grouse, Dudley the 74–5
Red and Yellow Barbet, Levi the 118–19
robins
    Robin the Robin 92–3
    Travis the Pink Robin 82–3
Roseate Spoonbill, Orlando the 62–3

safety issues 141
sewing 138–41
    order of sewing 139–41
    sewing in ends 138
Shalow's Turaco, Renée the 108–9

Silkie Chicken, Tricia the 84–5
slip knots 132
slip stitch chains 136
slip stitch to join into circle 132
slip stitch traverse in a ring 136
splitting rounds 131, 134
standard forms 8, 14–19
stitch markers 131
stitches, working 132–5
Stork, Ina the 36–7
stuffing toys 10, 138
Swan, Margot the 56–7

tails 137, 138, 140
Teal, Arthur the Blue-Winged 60–1
technicals 130–41
terminology, international 12
toes 16, 18
Toucan, Meghan the 90–1
treble crochet stitch 135
Turaco, Renée the Shalow's 108–9
Turkey, Ross the 66–7

Vulture, Emily the 72–3
Vulturine Guinea Fowl, Agatha the 120–1

washing birds 141
Wine-Throated Hummingbird , Pedro the 64–5
wings 19, 138, 140
    flapping 19
    flying 19
    ornamental 19
    soaring 19
Wood Pigeon, Dora the 34–5
working rows 134

yarn 10–11, 13
Yokohama Cockerel, Callahan the 126–9

A DAVID AND CHARLES BOOK
© David and Charles, Ltd 2025

David and Charles is an imprint of David and Charles, Ltd
Suite A, Tourism House, Pynes Hill, Exeter, EX2 5WS

ISBN-13: 9781446314999 paperback
ISBN-13: 9781446316054 hardback
ISBN-13: 9781446315002 EPUB

This book has been printed on paper from approved suppliers and made from pulp from sustainable sources.

Printed in China through Asia Pacific Offset for:
David and Charles, Ltd
Suite A, Tourism House, Pynes Hill, Exeter, EX2 5WS

10 9 8 7 6 5 4 3 2 1

Publishing Director: Ame Verso
Publishing Manager: Jeni Chown
Technical Editor: Rachel Critchley
Editor: Victoria Allen
Head of Design: Sam Staddon
Lead Designer: Rosie Collins
Photographer: Yantra Taneva
Stylist: Beth Plumbley
Illustrator: Evelyn Birch
Pre-press Designer: Susan Reansbury
Production Manager: Beverley Richardson

David and Charles publishes high-quality books on a wide range of subjects. For more information visit www.davidandcharles.com.

Share your makes with us on social media using #dandcbooks and follow us on Facebook and Instagram by searching for @dandcbooks.

Layout of the digital edition of this book may vary depending on reader hardware and display settings.